A HISTORY OF
FORD MOTOR
COMPANY

A HISTORY OF
FORD MOTOR
COMPANY

Marie Cahill

SMITHMARK

This edition published in 1992 by SMITHMARK Publishers Inc., 112 Madison Avenue New York, New York 10016

SMITHMARK books are available for bulk purchase for sales promotion and premium use. For details write or telephone the Manager of Special Sales, SMITHMARK Publishers Inc., 112 Madison Avenue, New York, NY 10016. (212) 532-6600.

Produced by Brompton Books Corp., 15 Sherwood Place Greenwich, CT 06830

ISBN 0-8317-4481-2

Printed in Hong Kong

10 9 8 7 6 5 4 3 2 1

Page 1: The car that made Ford Motor Company famous around the world—the Model T. This is a 1927 model, the last year of production.

Page 2-3: Ford introduced the legendary Thunderbird in 1955. Still produced today, the Thunderbird has always been one of Ford's shining stars.

**Designed by Tom Debolski
Captioned by Marie Cahill**

Below: The Models T's engine was a simple four-cylinder side valve unit. Note the three pedals. These were marked C, R and B. Pedal C (clutch) engaged one of two forward speeds. Pedal R—reverse—did the obvious, while Pedal B (brake) brought the car to a halt.

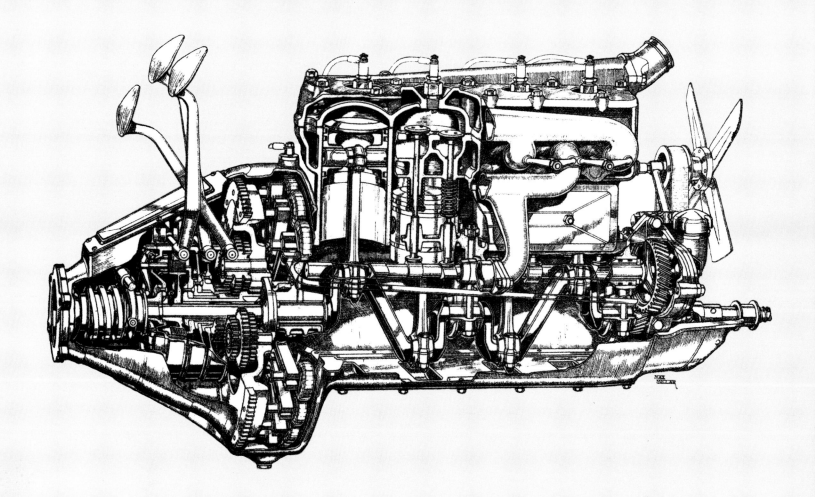

CONTENTS

HENRY FORD AND FORD MOTOR COMPANY

When he was 12 years old, Henry Ford saw a steam engine on a country road heading to Detroit, Michigan. Young Henry had seen steam locomotives on rails pulling trains, as well as the steam engines that powered threshing machines and sawmills, but never in his life had he encountered a machine such as this, never before had he seen a road vehicle moving under its own power—not pulled by horses. So intrigued was he by the sight of the road engine that he jumped off the wagon on which he and his father were traveling and ran to question the engineer about how this wondrous machine operated. Almost a half a century later, Henry Ford could still recall the conversation—and the chance encounter that became the inspiration for his life's work and dream.

Henry Ford was born on 30 July 1863 in Springwells Township, Wayne County, Michigan. He was the eldest child of William and Mary Ford. His father was born in County Cork, Ireland and emigrated to America in 1847 during the potato blight that ravaged Ireland. As he had in Ireland, William earned his living as a farmer, and by the time of Henry's birth, he was fairly prosperous.

Though he spent his youth on a farm, Henry personally had little use for farming. Instead, he was fascinated by the world of machines, and even though he hated the chores associated with farming, he was a master at repairing the tools and machines essential to the farmer. At night, Henry could be found tinkering with watches. At one point in his life, Henry contemplated making a dependable watch that everyone could afford, but he rejected that idea, reasoning that not everyone *wanted* a watch.

When he was 16, Henry left the farm and Wayne County for Detroit and an apprenticeship in a small machine shop that constructed steam engines. He was paid $2.50 a week—

one dollar less than his weekly room and board—so he fell back on his old pastime and repaired watches at night to make up the difference. Henry completed his apprenticeship in 1882 and began setting up and repairing steam engines for Westinghouse throughout southern Michigan. William Ford, Henry's father, preferred to have his son working the land, rather than as a machinist, so he offered Henry eighty acres of timberland. Henry returned to the countryside of his youth, but he also set up a first class machinist's workshop. With the lumber from his own sawmill, he built a home for himself and his future bride.

Henry Ford married Clara Jane Bryant of Greenfield Township on 11 April 1888. The couple first met at a New Year's Ball, held at the Greenfield Dancing Club on 1 January 1885. Henry and Clara lived in their 'square house' until 1891, when Henry took a position in Detroit with the Edison Illuminating Company, one of the several companies that furnished electricity to the city.

His lifelong aptitude for repairing machinery was readily apparent at Edison Illuminating. His first day on the job he repaired an engine stoppage that had baffled even the most seasoned engineers, and within a short time Henry had advanced to the position of chief engineer.

Though he excelled at his work for Edison Illuminating, his greatest satisfaction came from the time spent working on his own projects. Henry had never forgotten the road engine he had seen as a boy, and he was determined to build a self-powered vehicle. Henry's vision was shared by other inventors—Daimler and Benz in Germany, George Selden and the Duryea Brothers in the United States. Henry studied their work and at night he worked on a tiny vehicle—his own version of the 'horseless carriage'—in the woodshed behind his home on Bagley Avenue. His neighbors thought him crazy, but Henry persisted in

Facing page: Henry Ford and his first automobile, the quadricycle. He finished building it at four o'clock in the morning and immediately tore down the wall of his workshop so that he could get the vehicle out and take it for a test drive—in the pouring rain.

Ford continued to build automobiles in his spare time for the next three years, until 1899 when he, along with other investors, formed the Detroit Automobile Company.

his dream, and by June 1896 he had finished his first automobile. It was four in the morning and raining, but he took it for a trial run around the block—after tearing down a wall of the shed to get the car out. The next day, 'Crazy Henry' took Clara and their young son Edsel for a ride—much to the astonishment of the neighbors.

Henry completed two more automobiles by 1899, when the Edison Illuminating Company offered him an ultimatum—give up his hobby or quit his job. On 19 August 1899 Henry resigned, and, with the support of several

and the next morning Ford Motor Company was incorporated.

In addition to Ford and Malcomson, the stockholders were James Couzens, an employee of Malcomson; John and Horace Dodge, brothers who owned a machine shop; Albert Strelow, a contractor; John S Gray, a banker; Vernon E Fry, a real estate dealer; Charles H Bennett, an air rifle manufacturer; CJ Woodhall, a clerk; and Horace H Rackham and John W Anderson, lawyers. Much of the capital was in the form of shops, machinery, patents and so on, with only $28,000 in cash.

Below: *Henry Ford's workshop behind his home on Bagley Avenue, where he built the quadricycle.*

investors, formed the Detroit Automobile Company. Henry, who controlled one sixth of the stock, was appointed chief engineer. However, Henry and his supporters failed to see eye-to-eye, and within a year and a half the company was forced into bankruptcy. In 1901, Henry formed the Henry Ford Company, a venture that lasted only four months.

Meanwhile, Henry had been building cars—fast ones. On 10 October 1901, at the Grosse Pointe, Michigan track Henry Ford challenged Alexander Winton and his world champion car, 'The Bullet.' Three cars lined up for the 10-mile race, but only Ford and Winton left the starting line. After eight miles, Winton held the lead, but then his car began to sputter, and Ford passed him on his way to victory. Later, Ford designed his famous '999,' named after the New York train that had made a record run to Chicago. The car, which was driven by Barney Oldfield, a daredevil bicyclist, broke all the records at Grosse Pointe.

Right: *Henry Ford with race car driver Barney Oldfield in the famous 999 in 1901. Undeterred by Michigan's cold winters, Oldfield broke all records at the Grosse Pointe race track.*

Among those who saw the 999 cross the finish line a mile ahead of all the other competitors was Alex Y Malcomson, a wealthy Detroit coal dealer. A shrewd businessman, Malcomson understood that the production of automobiles could reap high profits. He met with Henry Ford on the evening of 15 June 1903,

Ford and Malcomson each had 25.5 percent of the stock in the company.

For its factory, the new company rented a building on Mack Avenue in Detroit for $75 a month. The building was only 250 feet long by 50 feet wide, but there was more than enough space because all the parts were manufactured at other sites and then brought to the Ford factory, where a dozen men assembled, adjusted and tested the finished product. On 23 July 1903 — one month after Ford Motor Company had been incorporated — the first car was sold to a Chicago dentist named Pfenning.

THE EARLY MODEL A

The first car built by Ford Motor Company was the Model A, or Fordmobile. Advertised as the 'boss of the road,' the early Model A had an 8-hp engine under the seat. Its two cylinders gave it a maximum speed of 30 mph, and its planetary transmission gave it two forward speeds and reverse. The wheelbase measured six feet, and the wheels were 28 inches in diameter, with wooden spokes. The crank was at the side, and a steering wheel, which was on the right, replaced the tiller that had been

used on earlier cars. There were no doors; the driver simply slipped into place behind the wheel. Though crude in comparison to the models that followed over the next several years, the Model A was efficient and lightweight, weighing only 1250 pounds. The Model A sold for $850. The tonneau, or detachable backseat, was $100 extra.

In the first nine and a half months of business, from June 1903 to the following March, the company sold 658 automobiles for a total of $345,190 and a profit of $98,851. The next three months were even more profitable, with sales reaching close to $650,000 in April, May and June of 1904.

The company, however, was not without its share of problems. Initially, customers complained that the Model A could not climb hills. Ford, the perfectionist, wanted to halt production until the problem could be solved. Couzens, who as secretary and treasurer handled the business affairs, realized that halting sales would lead to bankruptcy. The two compromised by sending out mechanics to the customers until the problem could be solved at the factory. In addition, radiators overheated, the carburetors were inefficient and the brakes failed. Ford Motor made so many adjustments on the Model A that in six months it was almost a different car. The Model A was, of course, far from perfect, but no one in 1903 expected a car to be completely reliable.

Perhaps the most serious problem confronting Ford Motor Company in the early years was the threat of a patent suit. In 1895, George Selden, a lawyer in Rochester, New York, had patented a self-propelled vehicle driven by an internal combustion engine. Seldon himself never built a car—and he was determined that no one else would either. In 1899, Seldon and his partners, a group of Wall Street investors, tried to enforce the patent against the five largest carmakers of the day, including Alexander Winton, designer of The Bullet. Rather than fight Seldon, the carmakers decided to join him and formed the Association of Licensed Automobile Manufacturers (ALAM). The carmakers had to pay royalties to Seldon, but they avoided what could have been a costly legal battle.

Ford Motor Company did not join the ALAM, and when the company started selling its Model A's, the ALAM warned the public not to purchase a car that was not manufactured under the patent of George B Selden. Ford responded with an announcement in the Detroit Free Press 'to dealers, importers, agents and users of our gasoline automobiles' promising 'We will protect you against any prosecution for alleged infringements of patents.'

In October 1903, the Electric Vehicle Company, the holder of the Selden patent, brought suit against Ford, the company's eastern dis-

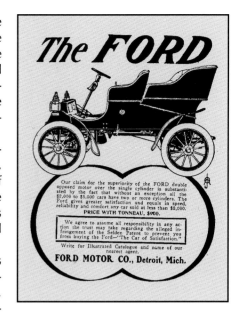

Left: *Ford Motor Company introduced its first car—the Model A—in June 1903. The car had a few bugs to be worked out, but sales were strong and the young company recorded a profitable year.*

Above: *An advertisement for the Model A. From the very beginning, Henry Ford was guided by the philosophy that everyone should be able to afford a car, and he priced the Model A at half the price of other cars.*

Left: *George Selden, in the driver's seat, and his brother Arthur. George Selden based his notorious 'Road Steamer' patent on this car. Hoping to corner the market on automobiles, George Selden compelled the major automakers of the day to join forces with him or face being sued for violating his patent.*

Ford Motor Company, however, refused to concede to Selden's demands and found itself embroiled in a major lawsuit. Ultimately, Ford won the case.

Below: *Henry Ford and the quadricycle. This photo, which was taken in 1896, was used as evidence in the Selden patent suit.*

Above: *With the cowling removed, the inner workings of the quadricycle are visible.*

tributor and the purchaser of Ford Car Number 134. A lengthy legal battle ensued and was finally settled in 1911 in favor of Ford Motor Company. At the time, however, the lawsuit had the potential to destroy the company. The threat of a lawsuit could have easily deterred the average car buyer from purchasing a Ford. Fortunately, Ford found a powerful ally in John Wanamaker, a well known capitalist who promised Ford customers they would be protected against the ALAM.

Henry Ford himself did much to advance his own cause. On 12 January 1904, in the bitter cold, he raced his 999 across the frozen Lake St Clair, covering a mile at the incredible speed of 39 2/5 seconds. The race attracted worldwide attention and drew people to a big automobile show held in New York's Madison Square Garden a few days later.

In its first 15 months, Ford Motor Company produced 1700 cars—early Model A's. The company began to experiment in an attempt to find the perfect car for the American public. The first 19 letters of the alphabet were used to designate Ford's creations, some of which were never seen by the public. In 1905, Ford introduced the Model B and the Model C, the former a $2000 touring car and the latter a $950 two-cylinder four-seater. Though they represented the opposite ends of a spectrum, both cars were inspired by European designs and had the engine up front under a hood, rather than under the seat. Each had its own innovations. The B had a 20-hp engine and automatic oiling, while the C had a back seat and a door.

The most successful of the early production cars was the Model N—a small, light, four-cylinder car that sold for $500. On the other hand, the Model K, a $2500 six-cylinder luxury car, sold poorly.

The Model K's failure, along with Henry Ford's insistence that the company's future lay in the production of inexpensive cars for a mass market, caused increasing friction between Ford and Alex Malcomson. As a result, Malcomson left the company and Henry Ford acquired enough of his stock to increase his holdings to 58 1/2 percent. Ford became the president in 1906.

By 1907, Henry Ford and his engineers had finished their experimenting. Henry Ford's vision was clear:

I will build a motorcar for the great multitude. It will be large enough for the family but small enough for the individual to run and care for. It will be constructed of the best materials, by the best men to be hired, after the simplest designs that modern engineering can devise. But it will be so low in price that no man making a good salary will be unable to own one—and enjoy with his family the blessing of hours of pleasure in God's great open spaces.

That car was the Model T.

THE BIRTH OF THE MODEL T

As president and controlling owner of the company, Henry Ford was free to pursue his vision of creating a simple, rugged and inexpensive automobile. The first Model T, 'homely as a burro and useful as a pair of shoes' was delivered to the first buyer on 1 October 1908.

The Model T was light and strong, in part because of the extensive use of vanadium and heat-treated steel wherever feasible. It weighed 1200 pounds, had a 100-inch wheelbase, and cleared the road by 10 1/2 inches, a fact that enabled it to triumph over the primitive highway conditions of the day. It was available on one chassis only, regardless of body style.

Propelling the Model T was a 20-hp, four-cylinder, three-bearing engine. The engine had a unique detachable cylinder head and a three-point suspension. A simple magnet built into the flywheel supplied current for ignition and lights. Power plant, transmission and rear axle were completely enclosed. The body sat high on transverse arc springs, and the roof rode seven feet above the pavement.

A pedal-operated planetary transmission, with only two forward speeds, enabled the driver to shift easily without danger of damaging the gears. This improved transmission was one of the Model T's most revolutionary features. Because the act of driving was still relatively foreign to most people of the era, many Americans simply did not know how to shift gears. The heavy clutches were difficult to shift, and the gears were easily stripped because the transmissions were made of a soft metal.

Capable of doing 45 miles an hour and delivering 20 miles per gallon, the Model T was believed by many to be able to go anywhere and do anything. A Ford bore out this theory in June 1909, when it negotiated the 4100 miles from New York to Seattle in 22 days under appalling weather conditions and over terrain where roads could hardly be said to exist.

The Model T was the first car that captured the heart and imagination of the American people. Nicknamed Tin Lizzie and flivver, the Model T could almost be called a national mascot. It certainly was one of the family to those who owned one. It was the first car to appeal to farmers, who hated the automobiles that scared their horses and ran over their chickens. Only a few years earlier, farmers had dug ditches and used logs as roadblocks against cars. Henry Ford, the erstwhile farmboy, was particularly pleased with the rural population's acceptance of the Model T. He had achieved his goal of designing the universal car, and was still looking for ways to ease the farmer's lot—the dream of a tractor was already brewing.

The Model T sold for $825, not as low a price as Henry Ford would have liked, but its cost was minimized in the company's advertising: 'No car under $2000 offers more, and no car over $2000 offers more except in trimmings.'

In creating the Model T, Henry Ford was assisted by a dozen engineers, notably Joseph Galamb, C Harold Wills, John Wandersee and August Degener. Galamb, a native of Germany, was the chief draftsman, under Wills' supervision. Wandersee and Degener developed the vanadium steel so crucial to the car's lightweight design. It was Henry Ford, however, who supplied the needed inspiration when a problem arose. He could look at the situation and suggest a change in the thickness of the material or in the distribution of weight. Ford may have lacked university training and an engineer's precision instruments, but he made up for it intuitively.

In order to fulfill Henry Ford's dream of the Model T, the company made plans to build a larger plant. Ford Motor had long since outgrown its original location on Mack Avenue. In 1905, the company had moved to a larger site on Piquette Avenue, but the production of the Model T called for something grander. Henry Ford therefore purchased the 60-acre High-

Facing page: Ford Motor Company launched the Model T on 1 October 1908. An unprecedented total of more than 10,000 cars sold the first year of production, a figure that multiplied year after year. At the height of its popularity in the mid-1920s, over two million Model Ts were sold in a single year. By the time production ceased in 1927, total sales exceeded 15 million units.

This 1910 Brewster green Runabout could also be had in grey. When production of the Model T skyrocketed, Henry Ford declared that customers 'could have any color of car they liked, as long as it was black.'

Above: *Immediately popular in the United States, the Model T's reputation soon spread beyond the nation's borders. The Model T was the first automobile to be sold in Turkey, Kuala Lumpur, Newfoundland, Barbados and Mauritius.*

Here, a foursome stops their Model T for a roadside picnic near Edmonton, Alberta.

land Park race track outside of Detroit. Construction of the new plant began in 1908, much to the amazement of the people of Detroit. The automobile still had limited appeal, and the average citizen could not comprehend that such a huge site could be devoted solely to building automobiles. Though the company was doing exceedingly well, the skeptics—including some employees of the Ford Motor Company—believed Ford's plan would be his downfall. The Model T, they reasoned, made sense, but for the company to devote *all* its energy into producing just that one car was, in their opinion, folly of the worse sort.

Highland Park was dubbed the Crystal Palace because of the more than 50,000 square feet of glass in the roof and walls. The four-story building was designed to make assembly of the Model T as efficient as possible. Raw materials arrived via elevator at the fourth floor, where the fenders, hood and other large parts were finished. Below, on the third floor, the floorboards were built, tires were placed on wheels and the bodies painted black. (Ford is famous for saying 'A customer can have a car

painted any color he wants so long as it is black.') On the second floor, the cars were assembled and then driven down a ramp past the first floor offices.

Henry Ford was guided by the principle that the design of the Model T should not be altered. Once the design had been selected, all the company's time, energy and efforts should be devoted to making the machinery to produce it, the idea being that as volume goes up, the cost per unit should decrease. Altering the design would entail retooling the factory and constant change would become the rule. Henry Ford believed that Ford Motor would better serve the public by concentrating on how to make the process economical.

When Ford Motor, as well as other carmakers, started making cars, everyone followed the same procedure. Cars were built one at a time. The chassis was placed in one spot until the car was finished as workers brought the parts to mechanics who assembled it. Later, assembly speed was increased somewhat by moving the cars along benches to teams of workers. Ford was using the methods implemented by the great industrialists of the late 1800s—Singer, McCormick, Colt. All of them contributed to what can best be described as the process line, a system that was based on a logical, progressive movement of the unfinished product. The process line differed from the assembly lines of today because movement was not continuous. The closest thing to a continuous flow was the system used by Chicago meatpackers in the 1860s. The meatpackers doubled their output by passing a hog carcass from worker to worker, as each one performed a single operation on the carcass, whereas before each worker had done an entire hog. Automation was not unheard of, however. In 1783, Oliver Evans created automatic conveyors to run an automatic grain mill he had designed and built.

The manufacturing process was also aided by the use of interchangeable parts, an innovation dating back to Eli Whitney. In 1798, Whitney used interchangeable parts to complete a rush order of 10,000 muskets for the United States government.

Henry Ford combined the basic principles and practices of these men into a single continuous process, refining them as he went along. Borrowing from Whitney, he made massive use, for example, of interchangeable parts so that unskilled workers could simply pick the parts at random and assemble them into finished products, thereby reducing the need for expensive skilled laborers. He experimented with gravity slides, conveyors, and the placement of men and tools for maximum efficiency. By dividing each manufacturing operation into its constituent parts, he multiplied the production of anything from flywheel magnetos to complete engines, often by as much as a factor of four. Department by department, Henry Ford established subassembly lines until, in his own words, 'Everything in the plant moved.' Ultimately, Ford created a moving final assembly line that started with a chassis without wheels and ended as a completed car,

Overleaf: *A 1910 Model T Runabout. By 1916, the distinctive brass windshield frame, headlamps and radiator shell were replaced with steel in an effort to keep costs low.*

Below: *Practical, reliable and, above all, affordable, the Model T suited city dweller and farmer alike. Henry Ford's dream of the universal car had been fulfilled.*
By 1916, the year this Tourer was built, the price of a Model T had fallen to $360.

driven off the assembly line under its own power.

In 1910, the first year of production at High-land Park, 19,000 Model T's rolled off the assembly line. The next year, the company produced 34,550, and by 1912, production had jumped to 78,440. In 1913, Henry Ford cut the price of the Model T to $440. Although profits per car went down (to $93 from $200), sales went up—from 78,440 to 248,307. As Ford explained, 'Every time I reduce the charge for our car by one dollar, I get a thousand new buyers,' and the demand for the Model T intensified as Ford continued to lower the price. The mass production capabilities of the Highland Park plant enabled Ford Motor Company to keep up with the demand, but more significantly Henry Ford's moving assembly line shaped the direction that modern industry would take.

With his Model T, Henry Ford had created a universal car; with the first moving assembly line, he advanced the industrial process. His next move would have an equal, if not greater, impact on industry. On 5 January 1914, he established the $5.00 a day wage—a figure that was unheard of in its day.

THE $5.00 A DAY WAGE

Prior to this monumental announcement, Henry Ford was neither generous nor stingy with the payroll. Workers received the going rate, which in 1908 was $1.90 for a 10-hour day. By 1913, the daily wage had increased to an average of $2.50. Henry Ford also paid his workers bonuses—albeit rather modest ones considering the dividends the stockholders were receiving. In October 1913, the company began to reform its wage structure and

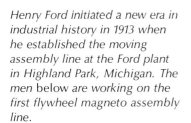

Henry Ford initiated a new era in industrial history in 1913 when he established the moving assembly line at the Ford plant in Highland Park, Michigan. The men below are working on the first flywheel magneto assembly line.

increased wages by 13 percent, with some workers receiving as much as $4.00 a day. At that time the auto industry was especially prone to a high rate of turnover. Companies typically laid off employees frequently, and in turn the employees naturally worked wherever they could find employment. Ford's wage increase in 1913 was intended to instill worker loyalty.

That increase, however, paled in comparison to the $5.00 a day policy. The new policy also changed the length of the workers' shift. Ford Motor Company replaced the two current nine-hour shifts with around-the-clock eight-hour shifts. For the worker, this meant higher pay for fewer hours, while for Ford Motor Company, the change resulted in increased production.

The new policy was not without a few conditions. The increased wage was, in reality, a profit-sharing bonus that employees were not eligible for until they had worked for the company for six months. There were also various other conditions that revolved around Henry Ford's views regarding how his employees should conduct their personal lives. Neverthe-

less, the $5.00 a day wage was an amazing event in the eyes of the public and the media. The *New York Evening Post* proclaimed it 'a magnificent act of generosity,' while the *Cleveland Plain Dealer* heralded it as 'a blinding rocket through the dark clouds of the present industrial depression.'

The announcement generated a tremendous response among the men. By two A M the morning after the wage increase was announced, men seeking employment had gathered in the freezing cold and snow outside Ford Motor Company. By dawn, their numbers had grown to 10,000. Within a week, men from throughout the Midwest had come in search of jobs. Fights inevitably broke out among them, and on the morning of 12 January—a week after the announcement—the mob turned on Ford employees as they reported to work. When the police arrived on the scene, they turned a fire hose on the unruly crowd, ending the demonstration with the bone-chilling water.

A week after the $5.00 a day wage was instituted, a reporter from the *Detroit Times* went to Highland Park to investigate the effects of

Above: *A group portrait of the crankshaft department at the Belleview, Michigan plant.*

Henry Ford took a paternalistic attitude toward his workers. Non-English speaking employees were required to take English language classes and everyone was paid in cash so that they wouldn't have to cash their paychecks in a local tavern and thus be tempted to have a drink.

this incredible policy. Though his report was glowing, all of Ford's workers would not have agreed. One such employee was Charles A Madison, a former Dodge worker who had been lured away by the fabulous wage. Much to his dismay, Madison discovered that he would have to wait six months before he was entitled to the $5.00 a day, and even at that wage he felt he could not work for Ford, with its strict production schedule. The end of his shift found him exhausted, as he could not take a break, even for lunch, if he was expected to fulfill his quota.

Non-English speaking employees—and they composed 71 percent of the workforce—were required to attend English language classes after hours if they wanted to receive their share of the profit-sharing, and the foreign-born employees who took time off to celebrate *their* religious holidays found themselves without jobs.

Women were not included in the $5.00 a day wage because, as Henry Ford explained, 'We expect the young ladies to get married.' Though this policy was changed, Henry Ford's view on the subject did not. In 1923, he told the *Ladies' Home Journal* that women were 'only a temporary factor in the industry. Their real job in life is to get married, have a home and raise a family. I pay our women well so they can dress attractively and get married.'

In spite of these drawbacks, the $5.00 a day wage had a far-reaching impact. Ford's English language courses did help immigrants assimilate into the population, and he hired more women and paid them a better wage than other Detroit companies. Overall, the $5.00 a day wage improved the life of the worker and set a precedent for the auto industry.

Henry Ford had first come to the public's eye with his victory in 1911 in the Selden-ALAM patent case. The lone man against the rest of the industry, the public viewed him as a folk hero, a role that was even more defined with the $5.00 a day wage. Eighteen months later, Henry Ford was again making headlines. This latest venture was a pilgrimage in the name of peace.

THE PEACE SHIP

The Ford Motor Company had been internationally known since 1903, when it sold its sixth car to Canada. The company soon established factories and agents in England, France and other parts of the world, and in 1912 Henry Ford, along with Clara and Edsel, visited one of the English plants. The trip made Henry very much aware of the perilous mood that permeated the world on the eve of the World War War I. Ford told the *Detroit Free Press* that he would rather burn down a factory than let it be

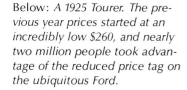

Below: *A 1925 Tourer. The previous year prices started at an incredibly low $260, and nearly two million people took advantage of the reduced price tag on the ubiquitous Ford.*

Above: *Model Ts like this 1921 Tourer came equipped with only what was absolutely necessary for it to operate, but extras—like oil gauges and shock absorbers— were readily available from various companies.*

Right: *A 1915 Tourer. On 10 December 1915, the one millionth Model T was completed. Up to this point, 64% of all Model Ts sold ended up in small towns or on the farm, but more and more would be sold for industrial use.*

used to produce cars for military purposes. He went so far as to say he would finance a 'world-wide campaign for universal peace.' Newspapers all over the United States picked up the story. Henry's opinions were read with interest by Madame Rosika Schwimmer, who presented herself at Highland Park on 17 November 1915.

Rosika Schwimmer, a Jewish Hungarian, was an active campaigner for peace and women's rights, but her aggressive methods had alienated her from pacifists who were more accepted by the general public, such as social worker Jane Addams, the founder of Chicago's Hull House. For her meeting with Henry Ford, Madame Schwimmer carried a huge purse, containing notes she had made during her conversations with the various heads of the European nations. Madame Schwimmer claimed that these notes were the proof that Europe wished to avoid a conflict and would welcome the intervention of a neutral party. Her objective was to have Henry Ford sponsor this undertaking.

To accomplish his goal of world peace, Henry Ford chartered a ship, the *Oscar II*, to send a delegation to Europe. Dubbed the Peace Ship, the mission was doomed before it started. Prior to departure, Ford, at a press conference, revealed that the plans for the delegation were vague and ill-formed. Once the Peace Ship had left New York, Rosika Schwimmer was generally uncooperative, particularly concerning her 'documents,' and seemed more interested in spending money, for herself personally as well as on a huge administrative staff. The delegates found themselves bored and at each others' throats. Ford was ill by the time they docked in Norway, and returned to the United States as soon as he was able. Henry Ford returned home expecting to be ridiculed for the failure of the Peace Ship. Instead, the public viewed him as a Don Quixote, a brave man who had tried and failed.

Shortly after his voyage on the Peace Ship, Henry Ford and his wife, Clara, moved into their new home in Dearborn, Michigan, 10 miles outside of Detroit. The Fords had been living on Edison Avenue in Detroit, but were constantly at the mercy of job seekers, reporters, fortune seekers and so on. With the break of dawn, there were people lined up outside their home seeking their attention. The situation became intolerable, and in 1914 Henry made plans to build a new home for his family.

Henry had originally planned to build in the exclusive Grosse Pointe area, where Detroit's elite escaped from the grime and congestion of Detroit's increasingly industrial inner city. Upon reflection, Henry realized he had no desire to live among the wealthy, though he could rightly be called a billionaire. The feeling was a mutual one, for the rich businessmen of Detroit had no use for Henry Ford and his $5.00 a day wage. Instead of Grosse Pointe, Henry opted for the woods of Dearborn on the Rouge River. Since 1908, Henry had been

Opposite, top: *An outdoor assembly line for the Model T, circa 1914. The carbody is dropped from a ramp on to the chassis.*

Opposite, bottom: *The Model T changed the way the world viewed the automobile. No longer a hobby of the rich, the automobile became everyday transportation for every man and woman.*

Below: *The Model T made its first appearance in Great Britain at the British Motor show in Olympia, London. It was an instant—and enduring—hit. During the show, 250 cars were sold, and the Model T would remain a best seller for years to come.*

buying land in Dearborn to build a bird sanctuary. If the area could provide his beloved birds with peace and quiet, it would suit him just as well.

Henry Ford named his new home Fair Lane, after the area in County Cork, Ireland where his grandfather Patrick O'Hern was born. Neither Henry nor Clara desired the trappings of the rich. Henry, in fact, had little use for money and Clara once found a check for $75,000 crumpled in his pocket. Nevertheless, Fair Lane was a huge mansion, with quite a number of amenities, ranging from a heated swimming pool to a private golf course for Edsel.

Edsel Ford was 22 when his family moved to Fair Lane. Henry and Clara adored their only child, and he loved and admired both of them. Edsel had been a part of Henry's enterprises since the very beginning. Henry had taken him along when he was just a toddler for test runs in the very first car he had made. When Edsel was eight, he was given a car of his own to drive to and from school. (At that time, there were no laws governing who could and could not drive.) Edsel had spent hours working with Henry in his workshop, and when he was in high school he worked at Ford Motor Company in the afternoons. In those days, he would come straight from school, leave his books on a desk in the administrative area and wander off to see what was going on in the experimental laboratories. The clerical workers began to notice that Henry would wander into their area every day late in the afternoon and scan the desks for Edsel's books. Once he spotted them, he would smile and head for the experimental section himself.

Though Edsel had the ability to continue his education at the best Ivy League schools, Henry distrusted higher education and wanted his son by his side. Upon his graduation from high school, Edsel started working full time at Ford Motor Company. In 1915, when he was 21, he was appointed to the board of directors and everyone assumed that one day he would run the company. Edsel could easily have become one of the privileged, a spoiled rich kid who expected to be given everything, but he escaped that fate. Edsel was well liked among the employees at Ford Motor Company. He was quiet, respectful and always concerned about the welfare of the workers. Though he would never wield the type of influence that his father had, Edsel would leave his own mark on Ford Motor Company.

Edsel Ford did not live with his parents at Fair Lane for very long. In June 1916, he announced his engagement to Eleanor Clay, the niece of Joseph L Hudson, founder of Hudson's Department Store. Edsel and Eleanor were married on 1 November 1916 in a quiet ceremony, much to the dismay of the local press, who desired a flashy event brimming with social luminaries.

Left: *In 1916, Henry Ford moved his family into a huge estate on the Rouge River in Dearborn, Michigan. True to his nature, Henry did things his way, preferring to live in the quiet woods of Dearborn rather than in Grosse Pointe, where Detroit's nobility resided.*

The new home was named Fair Lane, in honor of his grandfather's birthplace in Ireland.

ROUGE RIVER

By 1915, Highland Park was producing a quarter of a million cars a year and had the capacity to double that amount. Even so, the world's largest factory complex had become too small for Henry Ford. Having turned the production of cars into a science, he wanted to focus now on the raw materials that went into the cars. He had a vision of a giant plant turning out the rubber, wood and steel that produced the cars.

Henry also needed a larger plant to fulfill his plans to develop a tractor—an idea that had occupied a corner of his mind even before he had developed his first automobile. As a young man growing up in Wayne County, he had wanted to find a way 'to lift farm drudgery off flesh and blood and lay it on steel and motors' and had experimented with portable steam engines for simple tractor work. A few years after Ford Motor Company had been established, he told Joseph Galamb, one of his engineers, 'Joe, we have to have to build a tractor in three days.' Over the next several years, various models of tractors were developed, none of which were completely satisfactory. Finally, in 1915 Eugene Farkas began work on a model that looked promising. Henry Ford himself watched the project closely and realized that now was the time to make the move to a larger plant so he could pursue this project as well as expand the Model T operations.

By the summer of 1915, Henry Ford had found the perfect site for his massive factory complex in the marshes where the Rouge River flowed into the Detroit River. The stockholders objected to Henry's plan because it would require a tremendous amount of capital. The Dodge brothers were particularly concerned. Their company had been supplying Ford Motor Company with parts since the beginning, and they interpreted Henry's plan for a huge industrial complex as a loss of business. For the time being, Henry was forced to hold off on building his plant, but he refused to delay his plans to develop a tractor and formed

Right: The Highland Park facilities of the Ford Motor Company in 1927.

Built on a tract of land that encompassed 60 acres, Highland Park was the largest industrial plant of its time, capable of producing half a million cars a year. When it was built in 1908, the citizens of Detroit were amazed by its size, but by 1915 Henry Ford was making plans for an even larger complex.

a separate company, Henry Ford & Son, to produce the Fordson tractor.

The United States entry into World War I in 1917 provided Henry with just the opportunity he needed to finance his plant. The man who had earlier declared that he would rather burn his plants than produce materials for the military was now willing to build whatever the government needed to support the war effort. Highland Park turned out helmets, airplane engines, gasmaks and tractors for the military. The Model T was drafted as an ambulance, and Henry Ford even suggested encasing it in metal for service as a minitank.

Ford Motor Company was given the task of producing Eagle boats, the lightweight submarine chasers used to counter the U-boat threat. A new facility was needed to build the Eagle

boats, and the government became a willing—and paying—partner in Henry Ford's plan for a new factory on the Rouge River. Though some members of Congress objected to the government footing the bill for Henry Ford's latest project, they were placated with the suggestion that Ford might buy back the plant when the war was over.

Construction on the plant began early in 1918. Building B, as it was later known, was revolutionary in a number of ways. Not only was it the first time that ships had been constructed indoors, but the building itself was quite remarkable. Over a half a mile long, the steel-framed, hundred-foot-tall walls were composed almost entirely of glass.

On 10 July 1918, only eight weeks after it was begun, Ford launched the hull of the first Eagle

Far Right: *A Model T Tourer, for sale and still running some seventy years after it was built.*

Below: *A 1924 Model T doctor's coupe. Almost unchanged since its creation, the Model T's once revolutionary design was now obsolete.*

boat into the Rouge River. Inside Building B, the three production lines, each carrying seven boats, provided testimony of Henry Ford's brilliance, as well as patriotism. When the war was over, it was discovered that Ford's foray into shipbuilding was not quite as successful as it had seemed only a few months earlier. Of the 112 boats ordered, only seven had been completed and only one of those was actually in commission.

Henry Ford was quick to blame the Navy for the Eagle's production problems, and the boat's designers had indeed changed the specifications several times. Others laid the blame with Ford Motor Company. Making the transition from manufacturing cars to building

ships was more problematical than the engineers had anticipated. The glitches in the system were not worked out until the war was over, when Ford finally did deliver 60 boats to the Navy.

While Ford Motor Company was producing the Eagle, Edsel Ford was involved in a personal struggle with the military. When war was declared in April 1917, he applied for an exemption from military service, on the basis of his supervision of Ford munitions production. The draft board rejected his appeal, but fortunately for Edsel, a change in regulations classified him as 2-A, with dependents (his son Henry Ford II was born in September 1917), and 3-L, indispensable to a war industry. Edsel's

exemption prompted Congressman Nicholas Longworth to remark that of the seven persons in world certain to go through the war unscathed, six were the sons of the Kaiser, and the seventh was Edsel Ford.

National attention was focused on Edsel's draft refusal when his father announced his candidacy for the Senate. Two years earlier, Henry Ford had been a popular write-in vote in the presidential primary elections. In the Michigan primary, Henry Ford received 83,000 votes to Senator William Alden Smith's 78,000, and in Nebraska he nearly defeated Senator Albert Cummins. Ford did little, if any, campaigning. His folk hero image, combined with his recent Peace Ship voyage, was enough to

make him the people's choice. Finally, he endorsed Woodrow Wilson, lending advertising support that was crucial to Wilson's victory in California.

For the 1918 Senate campaign, Ford decided to follow a similar low-key approach. He made no speeches, issued no statements and spent no money on advertising. The end result is that he lost the Senate election, but by a surprisingly small margin.

By the time the election was over, Henry Ford had reached his fifty-fifth birthday. On 30 December 1918, Henry Ford made a startling announcement: He was resigning from the presidency of Ford Motor Company to build up other organizations. In his place, Edsel was elected president.

Henry and Clara left Detroit for southern California and an extended vacation, leaving Ford Motor Company and the rest of the world to wonder what Henry's next move would be. They didn't have to wait long. The headline of the *Los Angeles Examiner* on 5 March 1919 proclaimed 'Henry Ford Organizing Huge New Company To Build A Better, Cheaper Car.' According to the *Examiner*'s report, the new company would be in direct competition with Ford Motor Company. Henry Ford announced that the new company would hire four or five times as many employees as Ford Motor Company's existing 50,000 employees. He would build a plant in California, as well as numerous plants throughout the country. All across the country, Chambers of Commerce sent telegrams to Detroit extolling the virtues of their cities for Henry Ford's new company. The stockholders of Ford Motor were up in arms over the situation, as sales began to slack off while people waited for the new Henry Ford car. And that was exactly what Henry Ford had counted on.

Since 1916 Henry Ford had been embroiled in a lawsuit between Ford Motor Company and the Dodge brothers, two of the company's original stockholders. The lawsuit had its roots in Henry's plan to build his dream plant on the Rouge River. Henry Ford wanted to pour the company's profits into construction, but the other stockholders objected. Henry Ford then announced that the company's dividends, which had paid $60 million the previous year, would be restricted to $1.2 million, with the rest going back into production. The Dodges' 10 percent of the company would now be worth a mere $120,000 compared to the $6 million it had been worth previously. The Dodge brothers took the matter to court and won, and Henry, for the time being, was prevented from building on the Rouge River site. He appealed but the Michigan State Circuit Court found Ford Motor Company guilty of withholding dividends and ordered it to pay $19 million, plus interest, to the stockholders immediately.

Right: *The massive Rouge complex in Dearborn, Michigan. The plant was officially opened on 17 May 1920, when two-year-old Henry Ford II assisted his grandfather and lit Blast Furnace A.*

The Rouge consisted of over 90 buildings, with 229 acres of floor space, 30 acres of windows, 27 miles of conveyors and 93 miles of railroad track.

As the majority stockholder, Henry himself received most the dividends, but he didn't have control of the company—and that was what mattered to him. With Henry Ford's announcement that he was planning a huge, new company, some people began to suspect that the plan was merely a ploy to buy out the stockholders. Henry denied this, of course, declaring 'We will not buy a share of anybody else's stock.'

Meanwhile, Henry Ford, with Edsel's assistance, had been secretly buying out the minority stockholders, and in July 1919, Henry Ford become sole owner of Ford Motor Company, having bought the remaining 41.5 percent for $105 million. When he heard the news,

an elated Henry Ford danced a jig around the room, and Edsel told a reporter 'There will be no need for a new company now.' For his part in the buyout scheme, Edsel was given 42 percent of the minority stock.

Even as he was waging war with the Dodge brothers, Henry Ford was entangled in another lawsuit, a libel case he had brought against the *Chicago Tribune*. The case went to trial in May 1919, three years after the incident that had prompted the suit. In June 1916, President Wilson had called out the National Guard to squelch Pancho Villa's raids on the Mexican border. Henry Ford reportedly told his employees that anyone answering Wilson's call would lose his job. The *Chicago Tribune*

fact saved the jobs of the militiamen for them, and, moreover, had taken care of their families in their absence.

On the other side, representing publisher Robert R McCormick, was Elliot Stevenson, who had also handled the Dodge suit. Rather than focusing on the situation of the Ford employees, Stevenson turned the trial into an inquiry of Henry Ford's character. He was able to win a ruling from the judge that anything dealing with Ford's alleged anarchism, even if not related to the editorial, was relevant to the case.

When Henry took the stand, Stevenson wasted no time in unveiling Henry's ignorance of history. Though an engineering genius, Henry Ford had very little formal schooling. He didn't know when the American Revolution occurred, or who Benedict Arnold was. Henry Ford became the subject of ridicule in cartoons and editorials, but to much of the general public Henry Ford was just one of them. Like Henry, they were too busy working for a living to concern themselves with the details of the past. To the jury, Henry Ford had indeed been libeled. As one of the country's richest industrialists it seemed improbable that he could be an anarchist. On the other hand, the *Tribune*'s editorial had not caused him any financial harm, and they awarded him six cents for damages.

Throughout the trial, Henry Ford had maintained an air of casual indifference, but his indifference masked his inner feelings. He had been humiliated before the nation and would never again be the optimistic folk hero that had charmed the nation. He turned inward, to the company that was now completely his own.

By this time the Rouge River plant was nearing completion. Late in 1919 the coke plant was finished, and by early 1920 so was the sawmill. On the chilly morning of 17 May 1920, three generations of Fords—Henry, Edsel, and Edsel's young son Henry Ford II—assembled on the banks of the Rouge River. Two-and-a-half-year-old Henry II was assigned the task of lighting Blast Furnace A. 'The fun of playing with matches was almost too much for Henry II,' reported the *Detroit News*, but once the fire was lit both Henrys clapped their hands in delight.

Within a few years, the Rouge plant would be casting 10,000 automobile blocks a day. Its vast confines, composed of over 90 buildings, would consist of 229 acres of floor space, 330 acres of windows, 27 miles of conveyors and 93 miles of railroad track. Henry had acquired the Detroit, Toledo and Ironton Railroad, making it a crucial part of the plant. Rouge River employed 42,000 workers and needed a staff of 5000 janitors just to keep it clean. It was the greatest industrial complex the world had ever seen—a self-made monument to Henry Ford.

Left: A 1921 Model T center door sedan. The unique placement of the doors on this model allowed for ease of access to both the front and back seats.

ran an editorial that stated, in part: 'If Ford allows the rule of his shops to stand he will reveal himself not as merely an ignorant idealist but as an anarchistic enemy of the nation which protects him in his wealth. A man so ignorant as Henry Ford may not understand the fundamentals of the government under which he lives.' Henry Ford saw these as fighting words and brought suit for $1 million in damages.

The trial opened on 15 May 1919 in the small town of Mount Clemens, Michigan, which had been as selected as an impartial site. Henry's lawyers—he had hired eight of the states' finest attorneys—spent the first two weeks proving that the Ford Motor Company had in

EXPANSION AND DECLINE

In 1919, one in three cars was a Model T. In that year, Ford started including an optional self-starter, an innovation that made the people's car truly a universal car, for now women could easily drive the Model T. Ford Motor Company held a 40 percent share of the market and no other competitor came close. In second place was General Motors, composed of Buick, Oldsmobile and Chevrolet. There were a number of smaller, successful companies—among them Hudson, Studebaker, Packard—but their aggregate sales were not even close to those of Ford.

In 1920, however, the country entered a recession, and for the first time in the brief history of the auto industry, car makers understood the cyclical nature of their business. In times of prosperity, there was no stopping car sales, but when the economy slowed down, so did their sales. When the recession hit, the cash reserves at Ford were severely depleted by the Dodge case, the buyout of the minority stockholders and the construction of the Rouge plant.

Henry Ford's answer was to cut prices. He instructed his top executives to make reductions, but he rejected their recommendations, making more drastic cuts. The basic price of the Model T was cut from $525 to $360, the runabout went from $550 to $395, and the top-of-the-line sedan was lowered to $795. These price cuts, which were the most significant the auto industry had ever seen, forced Ford to produce cars at a loss, but Ford's competitors suffered even more. William C Durant, creator of General Motors, was compelled to sell out to the du Pont family. The price cuts helped Ford for a short time, but eventually sales dropped, as they had for everyone else. Ford Motor Company shut down for Christmas, as it always did, but it did not reopen until February 1921.

Henry Ford began making internal cutbacks. He reduced his office staff from 1074 to 528 and sold all the equipment the laid-off employees

Right: The Ford 2-AT was the first fruit of a business venture between Henry Ford and 'Jack-knife' Stout of the Stout Metal Plane Company. The 2-AT was the first all-metal aircraft in the United States.

had used, from desks and filing cabinets to telephones and pencil sharpeners.

The real solution to the 1920 recession was devised by Ernest C Kanzler. Kanzler was a good friend of Edsel and his wife, Eleanor. He was in fact married to Eleanor's sister, Josephine. A bright and capable young man, Kanzler was well-liked by Henry Ford too, and Henry had persuaded him to give up a career in law to work for him as a manager at Henry Ford & Son, the company that produced the Fordson tractor. When Ford had assumed full control of Ford Motor Company, he moved Kanzler to Highland Park.

While at the tractor plant, Kanzler had reorganized inventory after noticing how excess supplies took up space, as well as money. He modified the system so that raw materials were purchased only when needed. To save space, the freight cars that delivered the raw materials were also used to whisk away finished products immediately.

During the recession of 1920, excess supplies at Ford were valued at $88 million. Kanzler decided to ship out the supplies to dealers along with the regular shipments of cars. The agreement that Ford had with its 6000 or so dealers required them to pay for the shipment immediately. Now they were forced to pay for the spare parts, or if they refused the shipment, risk losing their franchise. Since they had done well by Ford in the past, most dealers chose to borrow money from the bank to pay for the shipments.

By the spring of 1921, Henry Ford had survived the postwar slump and boasted of hav-

Below: *The Ford 4-AT, affectionately known as the Tin Goose, was a 14-passenger corrugated metal aircraft. A number of US airlines purchased the Tin Goose and it had a major impact in the early development of the airline network throughout North America.*

Far right: *The successor to the 4-AT, the Trimotor 5-AT marked the end of Ford's involvement in the airplane business until World War II.*

ing gotten by without by borrowing from the bank. Ford dealers across the country knew exactly how he had managed such a feat. Henry had avoided borrowing from the bank, but he had certainly 'borrowed' from other sources.

However, not all automakers had managed as well as Ford Motor Company. In the fall of 1921, Lincoln Motor Company was on the verge of bankruptcy. Henry M Leland, the founder of the company, had a reputation for excellence in the auto industry. After manufacturing engines for Oldsmobile, in 1904 he became the head of the newly formed Cadillac Company, successor to the Henry Ford Company, which Henry had left in 1902. Leland, along with his son Wilfred, stayed with Cadillac after it was

acquired by General Motors until August 1917, when they formed Lincoln Motor Company to produce Liberty engines. After the war, the company introduced the luxurious Lincoln car, but public response, for a number of reasons, was dismal. Henry Ford entered the pictured in October 1921. The drama that ensued is somewhat tangled, as the Fords' story differs from the Lelands'. One thing is clear—Ford Motor Company did acquire Lincoln Motor Company in 1922. The Lelands stayed with the company for a time, but Henry Leland was as strong willed as Henry Ford and clashes between the two were inevitable. At one point, the Lelands offered to buy back the company but Ford refused. For a time it seemed that the two great car makers had resolved their differ-

ences, but the Lelands were soon on their way out, their positions assumed by Edsel Ford and Ernest Kanzler.

Edsel had always been interested in the aesthetics of car design and, in fact, had been an admirer of Henry Leland. With the acquisition of Lincoln, Edsel had the opportunity to pursue an area of his own interest. Henry could devote himself to his functional peoples' car, while Edsel could develop a high performance luxury car.

FORD TAKES TO THE SKIES

While the Ford Motor Company was in the midst of acquiring Lincoln Motor Company, Henry Ford was also pursuing another business venture. Fascinated with all things mechanical, Henry Ford had been interested in aviation for several years when he invested $1000 in William Bushnell 'Jackknife' Stout's Stout Metal Plane Company in 1922. Stout produced a series of all-metal aircraft, culminating in the Model 2-AT Air Pullman, which was designed with the help of George Prudden. The 2-AT, a corrugated metal high wing monoplane with a single Liberty engine, was the first all-metal airliner in United States. Metal planes were something new and were viewed somewhat askance by many aviation buffs of the 1920s.

Ford inherited this design when he bought out the interest of his senior partner, the erstwhile 'Jackknife.' Ford had been impressed with Tony Fokker's three-engined monoplane transport and dreamed of producing

something similar himself. He and Prudden, along with other former Stout Metal Plane engineers, experimented with several ideas, including the cumbersome 3-AT that Ford called a 'monstrosity,' before coming up with the 4-AT Trimotor. It was a 14-passenger, corrugated metal aircraft with a high full-cantilever wing of a type that was being used in Europe by Junkers, Fokker and others, but which generally had been ignored in the United States.

The Ford 4-AT Trimotor made its first flight on 11 June 1926. Nicknamed 'Tin Goose,' it sold for $42,000 and it sold fairly well, giving Fokker some stiff competition in the United States. Many airlines bought the 'Tin Goose,' and it made a major impact on the early development of the airline network throughout North America. Admiral Richard Byrd even used a 4-AT for his famous 28 November 1929 flight to the South Pole.

The 4-AT Trimotor in turn evolved into the

5-AT, a 14-passenger plane powered by a trio of Pratt & Whitney Wasp radial engines delivering 450 hp. The last of the 5-ATs, which sold for $65,000, rolled off the Ford assembly line on 7 June 1933, marking a total of between 194 and 199, depending on the source.

By this time, Henry Ford made the decision to abandon the airplane business after his friend Harry Brooks was killed in the crash of a Ford single-engine 'Flying Flivver.' Within two years the advent of the DC-3 made practically every other airliner in the world obsolete. Nevertheless, the Trimotor's reputation was such that Ford could well have developed a follow-on that could have competed favorably with the DC-3. Whatever undeveloped potential might have lain among the Tin Goose's unborn descendents, the old girl herself was so durable and reliable that large numbers were still flying well into the 1960s, and some are still flying in the 1990s.

Above: *Unloading the mail from a Ford Trimotor.*

Opposite, top: *Northwest Airways used the Ford Trimotor 5-AT for passenger and airmail service.*

Opposite, bottom: *This is an aerial view of the Ford Airport in 1931. A huge sign emblazoned on the roof of one of the buildings in the foreground reads: 'When possible land on runways.'*

Today, the Ford Dearborn Proving Ground occupies this site. The Henry Ford Museum and Greenfield Village can be seen in the background.

THE MODEL A AND BEYOND

As Ford Motor Company met the challenges of the early 1920s, Henry Ford continued to produce his people's car. In 1923, Ford Motor Company turned out 1,699,984 Model T's, and Highland Park was breaking production records. The company's closest competitor, General Motors, produced a total of 798,555 cars, of which 464,800 were Chevrolets. The following year found the auto industry in another slump. Sales for Chevrolet dropped 28 percent, while Ford suffered only a 15 percent setback and the Model T's future seemed secure as the 10,000,000th 'Lizzie' rolled off the assembly line. By 1925, however, Chevrolet was rebounding, whereas Ford profits declined by $20 million. Henry Ford, however, refused to believe that the people no longer wanted his car. He blamed the dealers, not his car, for the decline in sales.

By 1926, the evidence was too strong for even Henry Ford to deny. Ford production dropped by more than a quarter million, and the gap between Ford and General Motors began to narrow. Ford still sold twice as many cars as Chevrolet, but only two years earlier Ford had been selling *six* times as many cars. The price of a Chevrolet coupe was $645, and though a Model T sold for only $290, it lacked features, such as a self-starter, that were standard on a Chevy. The Model T's planetary gears, once revolutionary, were no longer needed on the smooth, paved roads, and, in fact, were a hindrance where speed was concerned. The Model T had not changed since 1908, which enabled it to be turned out in incredible numbers, but also contributed to its decline. The people of the Roaring Twenties wanted a more stylish car, a car that provided comfort and beauty.

In a last ditch effort to save the Model T, the car was given a facelift. The body was swung lower, the nose smoothed out and, in a complete reversal of previous policy, the Model T was now available in fawn grey, gunmetal blue, phoenix brown and highland green. It was all

to no avail. The day of the Model T had come and gone. On 26 May 1927, the fifteen millionth Model T rolled off the assembly line with Edsel behind the wheel and Henry in the passenger seat

The end of the Model T would also mean the end of Highland Park. The repercussions of the plant's closing echoed throughout the industrial United States. The auto industry used 18 percent of the nation's iron and steel, 74 percent of the plate glass, 85 percent of the rubber, 60 percent of the upholstery leather, 28 percent of the nickel, 28 percent of the aluminum, 24 percent of the tin, 15 percent of the copper and 19 percent of the hardwood. Ford Motor Company had, after all, turned out more than 50 percent of the country's automobiles.

With a net worth in excess of $700,000,000, Ford Motor Company was well equipped to handle the shutdown. The Fords themselves, according to a 1926 report in the *New York Times*, had amassed a fortune estimated at $1.2 billion.

For the last few years, Henry Ford had taken refuge at Greenfield Village. Once again he focused his energies on designing a new car. He wanted a car capable of delivering speed, power and comfort, a car made for the improved roads and the quickened pace of life. It would be longer, wider and more pleasing in its proportions than the Model T. Unlike the Model T, it would be available in a range of styles and an assortment of colors. The car would be named the Model A, after the first car produced by Ford Motor Company in 1903.

The design of the engine, however, proved to be the source of considerable debate. Finally, it was agreed that the Model A would be powered by a four-cylinder, 200-ci (3.3-liter), L-head engine, only a little larger than that of the Model T but developing 40 hp at 2200 revolutions per minute. It had aluminum alloy pistons and cylinder head, a three-bearing counterbalanced crankshaft and a battery

Facing page: *A 1923 Model T. Though the Model T was now at the height of its popularity, sales would decline over the next few years, and Henry Ford would be forced to admit that the era of his universal car had come and gone.*

The last Model T rolled off the assembly line on 25 May 1927, with Edsel Ford behind the wheel and Henry at his side.

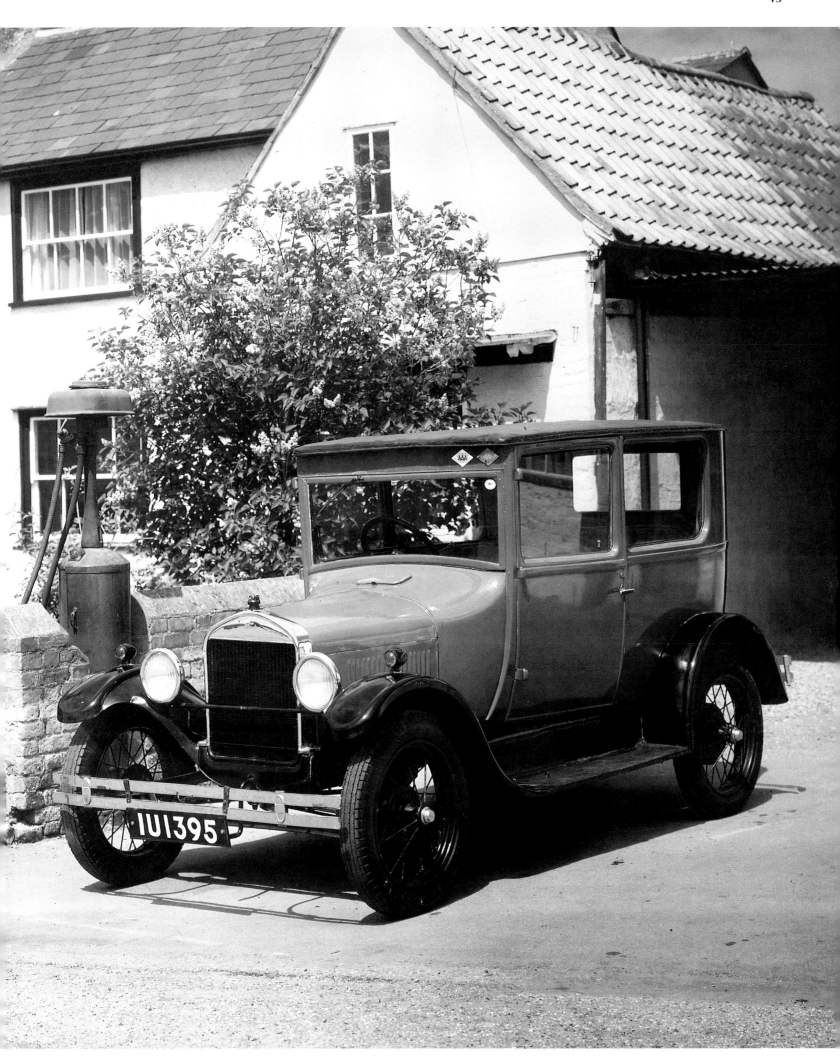

Opposite, top: Henry and Edsel with a 1928 Model A Fordor sedan at the New York Industrial Exposition.

Opposite, bottom: The unveiling of the Model A was greeted with an excitement unparalleled in the auto industry. By the time the first Model As were available, orders for the new car had reached 400,000—and not a single customer had even seen it!

distributor ignition. The outdated planetary transmission of the Model T was replaced with a three-speed sliding gear type, with gears of heat-treated chromium steel.

The Model A had a wheelbase of 103.5 inches, a tread of 56 inches and a road clearance of 9.5 inches. The steel body was lowered to reduce the car's height, but the weight—ranging from 2000 to 2500 pounds—was greater than that of the Model T. The Model A was available in Niagara blue, Arabian sand, dawn gray and gunmetal blue, while the Fordor sedan was offered in balsam green, copra drab, rose beige, and Andalusite blue. The car could be outfitted with wire wheels with steel spokes in contrasting colors. The Model A introduced such unprecedented features as hydraulic shock absorbers, safety-glass windshields, bumpers, automatic windshield wipers, tilt-beam headlights and a Bendix self-starter. The dashboard housed a gas gauge, ammeter and speedometer.

of radical new design were laid in place by the thousands. Factory space of 1.5 million square feet was added. A new method of electrical welding was devised to replace the old process of bolting the major sub-assemblies—a process that ultimately spread throughout the rest of the industry. In a reversal of his previous policy, Henry Ford purchased component parts—wheels, body panels, piston rings—from outside manufacturers.

The first Model A was completed in October, five months after the Model T was discontinued. During that time, 400,000 orders had piled up for a car that not a single customer had seen. By December a media blitz had created a public that was hungry for Henry Ford's latest car. The frenzy was heightened by delivering the Model A's to the dealers in canvas bags. Throngs of people were waiting for the Model A's arrival at dealerships, and in some cases, the press of the crowd was so great that showroom windows were shattered. Dealers in New York took in 50,000 cash deposits on just the first day the Model A was available, and an estimated 10 million people saw the car in the first 36 hours it was on display. The Model A was a celebrity, second only to Charles Lindbergh.

By spring of 1928, the lag between orders and available cars had jumped to 800,000. The scarcity of Model A's made them all the more popular. No longer was it an embarrassment to be seen in a Ford. Douglas Fairbanks was gladly photographed with the Model A he had given Mary Pickford for Christmas. He even telegraphed Dearborn to thank Edsel for providing them with the first Model A in California. 'It surpasses our greatest expectations,' he glowed. James Couzens, Henry Ford's former business manager who had left the company when he and Henry could no longer see eye to eye, requested the first Model A to be delivered to Washington. Edsel complied with his request and saw to it that the car was stamped with Number 35, the same engine number that had been on Couzens' first Model A when he was an accounts clerk for Ford Motor Company 25 years earlier.

Above: A 1929 Model A Tudor sedan. In contrast to its predecessor, the practical Model T, the Model A was regarded as an elegant and stylish automobile.

The Model A could reach a speed of 65 mph. Like the Model T, it could go anywhere and do anything in 20 miles to the gallon, but at far greater safety and comfort than its predecessor. Most incredible of all was the price. The Model A Phaeton sold for $395 and the Tudor sedan for $495—prices that were not much higher than the Model T and still less than a Chevrolet.

The retooling needed to produce this fabulous new car was phenomenal and of a scope never before seen in American industry. The Model A was composed of 6000 parts, almost all of them new, and their production entailed refurbishing the roughly 16,000 existing machine tools and building 4000 new ones. Highland Park's final assembly line was moved to the Rouge in September 1927. Machine tools

Henry Ford believed the worst was behind him and the new car would be produced for as long as the Model T. What he failed to think about was how much the auto industry had changed since its birth at the turn of the century. The Model A would face serious competition almost immediately.

Late in 1928 Chevrolet came out with a new six-cylinder model, competing with the Model A for the top spot in sales even though it was more expensive. The stakes were raised when Walter P Chrysler entered the race, who formed the Chrysler Corporation in 1925. While Ford was busy designing the Model A, Chrysler was hard at work selling DeSotos and Chryslers. When the Dodge brothers died,

Walter Chrysler acquired their company, which gave him the manufacturing capabilities to race headlong into the inexpensive market. He burst on the scene with the Plymouth and it immediately climbed to third place behind the Model A and the Chevrolet.

By 21 October 1929, Ford Motor had sold 1,815,000 Model A's, for a 34 percent share of the market, compared with Chevrolet's 20 percent. But three days later—on Black Thursday—the stock market crashed and ushered in the Great Depression, and sales for Ford—and all carmakers—declined. Over the next few years, roughly a third of all carmakers would fail, and in turn their failure led to the failure of a host a suppliers and wholesalers. With the success of the Model A, it appeared that Ford would continue to dominate the industry.

Above: *Bonnie and Clyde pose with their stolen 1932 Ford V8 Fordor Deluxe. A favorite among the outlaws of the 1930s, the V8, with its powerful engine, was America's first hot rod.*

Previous pages: *The smooth lines of this 1930 Model A Deluxe Roadster suggested an aura of sophistication. It was exactly the sort of car that the people of the affluent 1920s desired, and it gave Ford Motor Company the advantage it needed to reassert its dominance in the marketplace.*

However, with the advent of the Great Depression, all car manufacturers suffered. In 1930, Ford sold 1.1 million cars, while in 1932, only 211,000 sold.

Henry relied on his old strategy of reducing prices, but in 1931 sales dropped to 620,000. Ford Motor Company had lost its premiere position—GM had captured 31 percent of the market, while Ford dropped to 28 percent. Once again, Ford suffered because it had relied on one model.

THE V8

As he had five years earlier, Henry Ford created a new car, the V8—his last great innovation. Ford decided to produce an eight-cylinder after Chevrolet unveiled its six-cylinder. 'We're going from a four to an eight,' he told Fred Thoms, an assistant in the engineering labs. Engines with eight cylinders were nothing new. Cadillac had produced one as early as 1914, and by 1930 was even offering V12s and V16s. The difference was that these were individually made, premium cars with elaborate motor systems. Still guided by his philosophy of the people's car, Henry was determined that his V8 would be mass produced and affordable—and this was no easy task. In order for the car to be mass produced, the cylinder block had to be a single casting.

Fred Thoms examined every eight-cylinder engine he could find. All were made in two sections, some in three. After months of examination, Ford engineers developed a single-casting prototype, and by November 1930, they had a second model. For a year, they tested, produced and, on Henry Ford's orders, eventually scrapped over 30 engines. When Henry ordered 600 experimental pistons for a more conventional six-cylinder engine, it looked like the V8 project might be shelved. But Henry and Edsel met privately on 7 December 1931 and decided the V8 project would continue.

Charles Sorensen, the production head, estimated that it would cost an additional $50 million to proceed with the V8. Henry, who never objected to money spent on new machinery, told Sorensen to spend 'until it hurts.' Inspired by Henry's words, Sorensen commissioned a pouring furnace capable of holding two tons of molten metal as it moved beside the conveyor belt, filling the cylinder block molds as it went along. Sorensen also spent a sizeable sum on an electrical furnace needed to create the correct alloy mix that was so crucial to the strength of the single casting.

The V8 was unveiled in May 1932. During the first year of production, a few problems presented themselves but were ironed out. For example, lubrication problems resulted from the slant of the cylinders, causing the piston rings to leak after 1000 miles. The engine literally devoured oil, with some cars using a quart of oil every 50 miles. This problem solved, the V8 went on to become Ford's longest-lived engine. The V8 engines that Ford used in the

early 1950s were essentially unchanged since the engine's development 20 years earlier.

With the V8, Henry Ford again succeeded in his goal to produce the people's car. Priced from $460 to $650, the car was affordable, but the V8 was special—it was faster than all the other cars in the same price range. It was America's first hot rod.

Though the V8 was popular across the board, one segment of the population found the V8, with its powerful engine, particularly

appealing—the notorious gangsters of the 1930s. Between holdups, John Dillinger wrote Henry Ford 'You have a wonderful car. It's a treat to drive.' Clyde Barrow, of the infamous Bonnie and Clyde duo, sent Henry a tribute of his own: 'I have drove Fords exclusively when I could get away with one.' Clyde need not have written because the car spoke for itself. When Bonnie and Clyde met their inglorious end in the hills of Louisiana, they were driving a beige 'Desert Sand' V8 Fordor Deluxe. Stolen 7500

miles and 23 days earlier in Topeka, Kansas, the car was riddled with 107 bullets from the shotguns and rifles of the lawmen who ambushed them, but when the local Ford dealer was called to take the car away, the engine started the first time.

Henry had thrown himself into the V8 project with the same energy and enthusiasm that he had summoned for the Model A. By this time, however, he was close to 70 and his behavior was increasingly erratic. He threat-

Above: *Line workers at the Rouge assemble the 1931 Model A chassis. Production of the Model A required an almost complete retooling of the plant.*

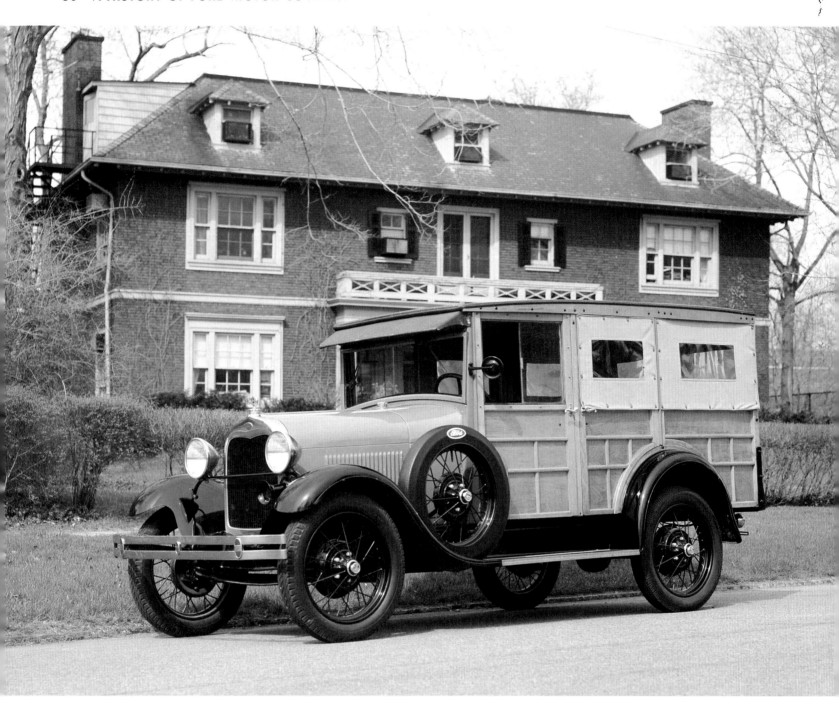

ened his designers and engineers, accusing them of selling his trade secrets to Walter Chrysler. On the other hand, when Alfred Sloan, head of GM, stopped by, Henry proudly took him to the engineering laboratory to have a look at the new engine. He puzzled his employees when he started wearing leather patches on the elbows of his jackets. The explanation was simple—Henry, the billionaire, just wanted his employees to feel that he, too, was feeling the hard times of the Depression.

As usual, Henry could be counted on to hold definite opinions. The hard times of the Depression, Henry believed, were 'a wholesome thing in general' after the excesses of the Roaring Twenties. Henry encouraged his employees, who could barely afford to buy groceries, to plant gardens and eat vegetables. Henry had also been opposed to philanthropy, believing that it weakened the spirit.

CRAZY HENRY

Until the Depression, Henry had been a hero of the common man. Now, however, his maxims about the human condition in the face of adversity wore thin. As a young man, they called him Crazy Henry. The name seemed to fit the man who thought vegetables would solve the problem of the hungry.

His eccentricities were apparent at home as well. He had always 'experimented' to discover the nature of things, but his experiments took a decidedly peculiar turn. His maid once found him boiling several pairs of socks. When she questioned what he was doing, he explained that he had always wanted to know why wool shrinks. He left old razor blades in the sink to rust and then used the water to wash his hair, believing that the rusty water was a hair restorative.

At the factory, the ventilation was poor because he believed that people with heart conditions or tuberculosis would benefit from exposure to monoxide gas.

He became fascinated by reincarnation. Once when driving along with an employee he explained that the chickens that had just scattered out of their path had done so because they had learned their lesson after they had been 'hit in the ass in a previous life.' He also told a cousin 'When a person dies I think their spirit goes into a newborn baby. I think that's why some people are so much further advanced in knowledge than others and are gifted. A man, when he dies, if he is a genius, his spirit will go into a newborn baby and that person will be an expert like Einstein or Edison.' Henry went on to explain that he had been a genius in a previous life.

Ford held strong beliefs about food, particularly as it related to health. Back in the Highland Park days, he had banned tobacco from the plant and discouraged his workers from drinking because his friend and idol Thomas Edison had warned him that these substances destroyed brain cells. He also rejected red meat. Once, in the Ford lunch room, he picked up a piece of white bread, rolled it into

Opposite, top: *The 1929 Model A station wagon was Ford's first wagon.*

Opposite, bottom: *The Model A differed from the Model T in almost every way. The out-dated planetary transmission of the Model T had been replaced with a conventional three-speed standard shift. In place of the bare bones interior of the Model T was an instrument panel with a gasoline gauge, speedometer, ammeter and ignition lock.*

Below: *A 1930 Model A Tudor, one of nine models to chose from. By the end of 1930, over four million Model As had been produced.*

Above and below: *Front and rear views of a 1935 V8 coupe. Like the Model T, the V8 was a milestone in the auto industry. While it was not the first car to be equipped with a V8 engine, it was the first V8 that was affordable for the average driver.*

a ball and hurled it at a window. When the glass shattered, he turned triumphantly to his astonished executives and proclaimed, 'That's what you're putting into your stomachs.' While many people today would agree completely with Ford's ideas, at that time they were the subject of ridicule. Some of his beliefs are still considered eccentric, even by the standards of today. Henry refused to eat chickens because they ate bugs, and he claimed that eating sugar was suicidal because the crystals would cut a person's stomach to shreds. He believed that cows would become obsolete because scientists would soon develop a synthetic milk.

Soybeans fascinated Henry Ford. He considered them a miracle substance and spent over $1 million in 1932 and 1933 researching soy-

beans. Some of his experiments yielded practical, industrial uses. Soybean oil was used in enamels to paint Ford cars and in fluid for shock absorbers, while the meal was used in window trim and horn buttons. The fiber from soybean protein was spun into textile filaments and used in upholstery. Ford even had a suit made from soybean wool.

Henry Ford found the dietary uses of soybeans more fascinating than the industrial applications and viewed soybeans as a universal food. At Chicago's Century of Progress exposition he had cooks prepare an all soybean meal: tomato juice with soybean extract, celery stuffed with soybean cheese, soybean croquettes as the main course, and for dessert there was apple pie with soybean crust and soybean coffee.

Perhaps Henry's most consuming project was Greenfield Village—his personal recounting of the past. 'History is bunk.' The *Chicago Tribune* attributed these words to Henry in 1916. Though he denied having said them, during the *Tribune* libel suit, he did agree that bunk was more or less what the school books provided. In the summer of 1919, after the trial was over, Henry decided to 'give the people a real idea of history.'

The project began on a relatively small scale with the restoration of the his birthplace. When a plan to widen the roads put his old homestead in danger, Henry Ford decided to move the building to a safe location and restore it to the condition it had been in when he was young.

A few years later, he found himself involved in another restoration project. In 1923, a group of Bostonians approached him to contribute to a fund to save the Wayside Inn at South Sudbury, Massachusetts. The inn, where George Washington and Lafayette had once stayed, had been made famous by Henry Wadsworth Longfellow. Built in 1686, the Wayside Inn was believed to be the oldest working tavern in the United States.

Henry never was one for contributions, so he purchased the Inn and undertook the restoration project himself, using men from the Ford plants to do the work. He opened 16 sealed fireplaces and tracked down as much as he could of the original furniture. So that the inn would be set in the same type of environment as it had been in the past, he purchased 2500 surrounding acres and began the task of turning back the clock. Ironically, automobiles— the source of his wealth—belonged to neither the time nor place of the Wayside Inn, so he spent $280,000 to divert the road which ran in front of the inn.

Henry decided to recreate a colonial village around the Wayside Inn and began transporting antique buildings from other parts of New England to South Sudbury. A treasured find was the old schoolhouse attended by Mary

Elizabeth Sawyer, who 'had a lamb with fleece as white as snow.' Whether Mary did indeed have such a lamb never mattered to Henry.

He then turned his attention closer to home and began devoting a major part of his time, energy and money to bringing historical buildings and artifacts to Dearborn and Greenfield Village. He brought the jewelry shop where he had once repaired watches and the shop in which he had built his first automobile, later adding his already restored birthplace. But Greenfield Village was not just a monument to the past of Henry Ford. He also included the Menlo Park laboratory of his idol Thomas Edison, a seventeenth-century stone cottage from England, the house where songwriter Stephen Foster was born (it was later discovered that Foster was *not* born there), an early American glassworks, a steamboat from the Suwannee River and a Cape Cod windmill, among other things. Though it may seem like an odd collection of buildings, every item had belonged to the world of the working man, and the buildings once again became part of the working world. Many Ford employees sent their children to one of the four schools in Greenfield Village.

Henry visited Greenfield Village daily. From the blast furnaces of the industrial colossus, the Rouge, he turned to the peaceful surroundings of Greenfield Village. He sat in the chairs, climbed the stairs, and ate the food from the kitchens of the old time structures.

Greenfield Village is a celebration of rural America. Next to it is the Henry Ford Museum, a collection of engines and mechanical devices offering tribute to the modern machine. The exterior of the building is a full-scale, red brick replica of three buildings that played a crucial role in American history: Independence Hall, Congress Hall and the Old City Hall in Philadelphia. Inside are steam engines, like the ones that Henry repaired as young mechanic, and Ford cars dating all the way back to the Quadricycle, Henry's first car.

As one of the first examples of living history, Greenfield Village provided an innovative, but also serious study, of history. Freed from the constraints of dates, wars, and the kings and queens that Henry Ford so objected to in textbooks, Greenfield Village captured a piece of the past, but *only* a very small piece, and it was a past that appealed to the whim and fancy of Henry Ford.

Above: *A 1935 V8 Fordor touring sedan. Henry Ford had done it again – Ford Motor Company sold one million V8s in 1935.*

Overleaf: *The brilliant green paint used on this V8 Fordor touring sedan was Ford's spring season color for 1936.*

EDSEL FORD

On 18 December 1918, Edsel Ford was appointed president of Ford Motor Company, a position he would hold until his death. The first task performed by the newly appointed president was the buyout of the minority stockholders. It was a task entrusted to him by his father while Henry was in California, supposedly building up a new company. Edsel succeeded in buying out the minority stockholders, and the company truly became a family company, with Edsel holding 42 percent of the stock, Henry 55 and Clara three.

After resigning the presidency, Henry Ford held only a position on the board and ostensibly let Edsel run the company. The reality is that Henry was never able to surrender the reins of power, nor was Edsel able to seize them. Edsel's tenure as president was marked by Henry countermanding his plans and orders. Henry and Edsel had, of course, disagreed on the Model T, with Henry unwilling to end the production of his beloved little car. In the early 1920s, Edsel made plans to build a new office building to accommodate the growing sales and accounting staffs. Henry objected to the plan and retaliated by firing the entire accounting staff. Over the next few weeks, Edsel found a new position somewhere in the Ford organization for every one of the dismissed employees. The odd thing is that Henry knew exactly what Edsel was doing. On another occasion, Edsel ordered a new line of coke ovens for the Rouge plant. On the surface, Henry appeared to agree with the plan, but he secretly planned to tear them down as soon as they were completed, and that is exactly what he did.

As the situation at Ford Motor Company became more difficult for Edsel he turned inward, and as if to make up for the ills in his relationship with his father, Edsel was determined to be a good father himself. Edsel and Eleanor's firstborn, Henry II, was followed by another son in 1919. Originally named for his father, Edsel Junior was renamed Benson. Josephine was born in 1923, and two years later William Clay arrived. The year of Josephine's birth, the Edsel Fords bought a country estate, Haven Hill, north of Detroit. Most weekends found the family at Haven Hill riding horses, swimming, or playing tennis.

Vacations were spent in exclusive Hobe Sound, near Palm Beach, Florida, or at Seal Harbor, Maine, where the family, along with an entourage of horses and servants, arrived via private railcar.

The Edsel Fords had a happy and comfortable, but definitely aristocratic, lifestyle. They employed nannies, cooks and housekeepers. As president of Ford Motor Company, Edsel Ford commanded a yearly salary averaging $3 million. They enjoyed their wealth, but Edsel's attitude toward philanthropy differed notably from that of his father's. After meeting Franklin Roosevelt at Palm Springs, Edsel wrote an unsolicited check to FDR for $25,000 for a foundation to fight infantile paralysis.

Edsel and Eleanor were also collectors of fine art, and throughout the 1920s and 1930s, the couple became two of the most discriminating patrons of art in North America. Edsel made significant contributions to Detroit's art museum, the first of which was a rare sixteenth century Isfahan carpet to celebrate his appointment as a trustee of the Arts Commission. Though the museum had been established since 1885, the quality of its art had declined in recent years. Through the generosity of the Edsel Fords, the Detroit Institute of Arts rose to a place of prominence as one of the leading museums in North America. Edsel was also a founding patron of the Museum of Modern Art in New York, one of the few who lived outside of New York City.

Perhaps Edsel's finest contribution to the arts was a gift given to the city of Detroit in the midst of the Depression—a gift that not only captured the strife of those painful years but also provided a testimony to the vision and

Above: *Ford lost its sales lead to Chevrolet during the Great Depression, but the company rebounded in the late 1930s thanks, in part, to cars like this 1937 V8 Fordor sedan.*

Previous pages: *A 1936 V8 Country Squire Wagon. The V8 was available in four body styles, of which the Tudor was the most popular.*

genius of Henry Ford. Dr William Valentiner, Edsel's mentor and the director of the Detroit Institute of Art, envisioned a mural on the inner walls of the museum's central courtyard. It would depict the heart and soul of the city — the automotive industry — and Valentiner knew exactly the man for the job. He was Diego Rivera, a Mexican artist of some renown on the European-American art circuit. Rivera's style blended primitivism with an appreciation of modern machinery and manufacturing. Edsel, now president of the Detroit Institute of Art, supported the project wholeheartedly, contributing additional funds.

The completed work of art covered every inch of the museum's central courtyard. In the center of the fresco are V8 workers toiling at their task, while above them four giants, representing the Indians, Caucasians, Asians and Blacks that shaped North America, sift through sand, salt and rock. Henry and Edsel Ford are featured in the fresco, as are workers picking up their wages. Other panels illustrate the peaceful and destructive sides of technology — chemical warfare is contrasted with medical research and war planes are seen next to passenger planes.

The people of Detroit were outraged when the fresco was finally unveiled. They resented paying what was rumored to be an excessive sum of money to a foreign artist and lamented the loss of the peaceful, restful courtyard — the one place that had been an oasis in a desert of smokestacks. Public sentiment called for the frescoes to be removed or whitewashed. Edsel Ford stood firm. 'I admire Mr Rivera's spirit,' he said. 'I really believe he was trying to express his idea of the city of Detroit.'

While Diego was painting his testimony to the working class virtues of Detroit, Edsel was involved in a personal financial crisis. Just before the Depression, Edsel became involved in the Guardian Detour Union Group, Inc, a holding company of banks. As the Depression continued into 1931, the Guardian needed a $15 million emergency loan from the Continental and other banks. The loan was made possible because Edsel put up the security. By the start of 1932, the Guardian owed Edsel $8.5 million, which it was completely unable to pay, as the trust had only $6 million in assets against $20 million in liabilities.

The situation grew worse for the Guardian, as well as the other banks in Detroit. The Commerce Secretary, Roy D Chapin, had approached Henry Ford, requesting his assistance. Ford refused outright, declaring 'Let them fail! Let everybody fail! I made my fortune when I had nothing to start with, by myself and my own ideas. Let other people do the same thing. If I lose everything in the collapse of our financial situation I will start at the beginning and build it up again.' Three days later the governor of Michigan declared a bank holiday. The 436 banks and trust companies were to be closed for a week until a solution to the problem could be found. After a week, the banks remained closed.

Detroit was almost without money. Those people who had cash on hand before the banks closed rushed out to the grocery stores and cleared the shelves. The city defaulted on its own bonds and issued its own money, which could be turned in for real cash as soon as money became available.

Edsel Ford felt certain he was on the verge of being wiped out. Fearful of making any other financial commitments, the typically generous Edsel had refused to loan to his friend Admiral Richard Byrd a Ford Trimotor plane for another expedition to the Antarctic. He laid off all but four of the 24 employees on his estate. Edsel had been unwilling to go to Henry for his help, but Henry found out about Edsel's predicament and bailed him out. Afterwards, Henry just happened to run into Edsel and casually remarked, 'Well, son, I see they took you to the cleaners.'

By this time, Henry was nearing 70, an occasion that by rights should have signalled a willingness to hand control over to Edsel. The banking fiasco made it clear that he intended to continue to rule. With Henry still running the show, Edsel needed other avenues to explore, which is why the acquisition of the Lincoln Motor Company was beneficial to Edsel on a personal level. Edsel had his own design studio in the old Lincoln plant, and there he could relax and work on designs for the aristocratic Lincoln.

LINCOLN AND MERCURY

'Father made the most popular car in the world,' Edsel once mused. 'I would like to make the best.' To that end, he hired John Tjaarda, one of the designers behind the stunning Dusenbergs and Packards. In 1935, Lincoln introduced the Zephyr, which the Museum of Modern Art called 'the first successfully designed streamlined car in Amer-

Below, from top to bottom: A 1939 Ford Deluxe coupe and a 1936 Lincoln Zephyr.

The Zephyr was developed under the direction of Edsel Ford, whose goal was to develop the 'best car in the world.'

Right: *Powered by a side-valve V12 engine, the stylish Lincoln Zephyr was well-received by industry critics and the car-buying public alike. This is a 1936 Model 902.*

Below: *A 1937 Lincoln Zephyr sedan. The popular four-door sedan was one of 12 body styles. The Zephyr introduced the concept of a streamlined car to the American public, and its shape would influence car design into the 1950s.*

ica.' The Zephyr had a 122-inch wheel base and a 110 hp motor. Priced at $1275, it gave Ford an entry into the medium-price field. Sales were encouraging. Two years before only 2170 Lincolns had been sold, and by 1936 sales had jumped to 18,994 Lincolns, of which 17,715 were Zephyrs.

Edsel also played a major role in the development of the Mercury, a car designed to compete with Pontiac and Dodge in the medium price field. The Mercury was conceived as a lower medium-priced car, filling a niche between the Ford car and the Zephyr. The Ford ranged in price from $540 to $920, the Mercury (in five types) from $920 to $1180, and the Zephyr sold for $1360 and up. Sales Manager John Davis devised an elaborate marketing plan for the Mercury. Salesmen were to be hired specifically for the Mercury and a service organization set up to handle the questions and complaints of Mercury owners.

Prior to its November release, the Mercury received considerable attention when Ford announced that the new car would have a wheel base of 116 inches, compared to 112 for the DeLuxe V8, and be equipped with the most powerful V8 engine to date. Ford's announcement also lauded the Mercury's flowing lines, wide and roomy interior and luxurious upholstery.

In 1939, Edsel unveiled his ultimate achievement—the Lincoln Continental. Sleek and low-slung, it was *the* classic car in an era of classic cars. With its 12-cylinder engine, the Lincoln provided a smooth 'glider-ride.' With its trademark spare tire on the rear, the car was so beautiful that Edsel immediately drove it to Florida to show it off. He had intended to produce only three cars, one for himself and one each for his sons, Henry II and Benson, but by the time he returned from Florida 200 orders had come in from people who had seen the Continental on the road.

Henry Ford, however, was less than impressed, taking little interest in 'motors that had more spark plugs than a cow has teats.' Regarding the Lincoln as a mere plaything of Edsel's, Henry resisted putting money into its production and the car never rose above the status of beautiful loser.

FORD AND THE LABOR MOVEMENT

Henry and Edsel differed philosophically on how the company should be run. Edsel recognized that Alfred Sloan at General Motors was setting the prototype for a modern corporation. Sloan had developed a decentralized form of management, with the automotive divisions functioning as independent units but working together as part of a joint effort. New fields, such as finance, became integral to GM's well-being, and emphasis was given to long-range planning. Sloan's ideas about corporate organization were as revolutionary as Henry Ford's dream for the automobile had once been, but Henry was unwilling to accept Edsel's proposals for reorganizing Ford Motor Company.

As the differences between Henry and Edsel intensified, Henry's harassment of Edsel increased in an effort to 'toughen up' Edsel. He perceived his son as weak and believed that countermanding Edsel's plans was actually beneficial to his son. Henry used a form of 'sibling rivalry' as a means of toughening up Edsel, turning first to Charles E Sorensen as a surrogate son. Born in Denmark, Sorensen had immigrated to the United States with his family when he was four years old. He first met Henry Ford in 1902, before Henry had established Ford Motor Company. Henry was impressed with Sorensen and promised him a job as soon as he started his new company. True to his word, Henry Ford hired Sorensen when he opened the Mack Avenue plant. Sorensen quickly established himself as a visionary in production and was in fact instrumental in developing the assembly line at Highland Park. Sorensen eventually sought control of the Rouge and in order to gain that position allowed Henry to pit him against Edsel. Once Sorensen had what he wanted he backed away from the conflict between father and son. Meanwhile, Harry Bennett was waiting in the wings to assume the part that Sorensen had abdicated.

Bennett was 24, just a few years older than Edsel, when he started with Ford Motor Company in 1917. Short, square-jawed and pug-nosed, Harry first worked on the Eagle boat project. His pugnacious personality did not escape Henry Ford's attention, and he was soon promoted to head watchman at the Rouge, where he became Sorensen's right hand man and willing participant in any situation that might be dangerous.

Bennett formed the Service Department, which performed service functions but also roamed the Rouge, keeping an eye on the workers. He became Henry Ford's henchman. Edsel and the other executives saw Bennett as the resident tough guy at Ford Motor Company and not the sort to challenge their authority, but ironically it was his belligerent personality that gave him an inroad to power within the company. Harry Bennett and his Service Department were appointed as the personal bodyguards of the Ford family following the kidnapping of the Lindbergh baby in 1932.

The Fords received a threat from a man who said he would kill all of Edsel Ford's children if he were not paid a ransom. Bennett arranged for one of his men to pose as Edsel Ford and supposedly deliver the ransom to the designated spot, a church. Bennett's men grabbed the extortionist when he went into the church to pick up the ransom, worked him over and *then* called the police. Bennett handled a number of similar episodes with the same style. Bill Ford, Edsel's youngest son, later recalled the time he and Henry II had been threatened. 'Bennett said he'd handle it. Later on, the guy was found floating face down in the river.'

Bennett's rise to power was fortified by his part in the labor unrest triggered by the Depression. The company that had once been commended for instituting the $5.00 a day wage was now under attack for its treatment of workers. In March 1932, Communist orga-

nizers arranged a 'March on Hunger' through the streets of Detroit to Dearborn and the Rouge. As the crowd headed for Ford's employment offices, the Dearborn police tried to stop them with tear gas, but strong winds blew the gas back in their faces. Fire trucks doused them with water but still the crowd marched on. When the demonstrators reached the Rouge, Harry Bennett rushed out to the front gate to talk with the leaders. Bennett began arguing with Joseph York, the 19-year-old leader of the Young Communist League, and the crowd responded by throwing bricks at Bennett. As Bennett fell to the ground, he pulled York down with him. When York stood up he was greeted with machine gun fire and fell to the ground, dead. Three other men were killed and 20 more injured.

Bennett was knocked unconscious and had to be hospitalized. While in the hospital, Henry Ford called him every day to check on his progress and sent him a Lincoln as a reward for his bravery. When Bennett was released from the hospital, he returned to an increased budget for the Service Department, and as he began to build up an army of ex-hoods accountable only to him his influence continued to grow.

As the Depression persisted so did labor unrest. The Detroit auto workers were among the best paid group of workers in the world, and the automakers had therefore managed to keep unions out of the shops. Labor organizers did little to advance their own cause. The existing labor organizations were dominated by guild and craft unions and tended to look down on the mass production worker of the auto industry. In the 1920s, the American Federation of Labor had attempted to organize the auto workers, but squabbling amongst the various craft unions of which the AFL was composed derailed the attempt. Finally, in 1935, the mass production workers, fed up with the domination of the crafts unions, left the AFL, eventually forming the Congress of Industrial Organizations. In April 1936, the car workers agreed to affiliate with the CIO and the United Auto Workers Union was born.

Realizing that Ford Motor Company posed the greatest challenge, the UAW decided to begin with GM and staged a series of sit-in strikes in the early months of 1937, and by February GM had agreed to negotiate with the union. The UAW then focused its energies on Chrysler, achieving the same success as it had at GM. The UAW was ready to take on Ford Motor Company.

Henry Ford was adamantly opposed to the union; Edsel believed that unionization was inevitable and urged his father to participate in collective bargaining. The two of them argued bitterly about the issue, and Charles Sorensen was so dismayed by their clash that he left the room. Henry finally settled the debate one afternoon when he met with Edsel and Sorensen and told them he had picked the man to deal with the union: Harry Bennett.

Edsel did what he could to let the union know he was sympathetic to their cause, but against Bennett and his army he had no say in the matter. Bennett had increased the Service Department's power and tightened security at the Rouge, and indeed his tactics seemed to be working, for the UAW did not find the same success they had at GM and Chrysler.

In May 1937, the union applied to the Dearborn City Council for a license to distribute pamphlets at the main gates of the Rouge plant. Under the Wagner Relations Act of 1935, which guaranteed this right, the city council had little choice in the matter. On the morning of 26 May 1937, the demonstrators gathered at the overpass connecting the parking lot on one side of Miller Road with the Rouge on the other.

One of the leaders of the demonstrators was Walter P Reuther, a former Ford employee. A brash 20-year-old from West Virginia, Reuther had started at Ford as a tool-and-die leader—an elite position usually reserved for those with 20 years of experience at the craft. When he tried to organize his fellow workers, he found himself out of a job and blacklisted with the other Detroit car makers. Undaunted, Reuther went abroad and obtained a position as a tool-and-die leader at a Ford-assisted factory in the Soviet Union. Back in Detroit, he used an alias to find employment and had been a strong participant in the labor movement.

Right: *To car enthusiasts today, the styling of the 1940 Ford Deluxe coupe, with its crisply pointed hood and curved fenders, is nothing short of marvelous.*

Below: *A 1940 Deluxe delivery wagon. The 1940 Ford had a 112-inch wheelbase and a choice of either a 60 hp or an 85 hp L-head V8. The V8/85, which was available in a wider range of models and trims, was by far the more popular choice.*

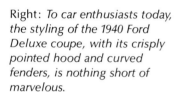

On that spring afternoon, Reuther was joined by Richard Merriweather, Ralph Dunham and Richard Frankensteen. As the four of them approached the overpass, they were met by Bennett's men. Reuther was greeted with a sharp crack across the back of his head. He went down and was kicked in the face. He was picked up, smacked again, thrown down and then picked up again to have the ordeal repeated. Richard Frankensteen's coat was used against him as a strait jacket, leaving him helpless. The other two activists received similar treatment. It would have been a complete and ugly victory for Bennett were it not for the press, who captured the event on film. The images of the bloodied and beaten Reuther and Frankensteen became a symbol of the struggling labor movement.

Ford Motor Company fought off the UAW for the next three years, and the ensuing battles between Edsel and Harry Bennett took their toll on Edsel, emotionally as well as physically.

By the end of his thirties, Edsel's health was declining. He was susceptible to colds and increasingly plagued by stomach problems. Bennett never challenged Edsel directly; instead he would go to Henry seeking support.

One of Edsel and Harry's most serious differences revolved around John Davis, the general sales manager. In 1939, Davis went to Edsel with a complaint about Harry Mack, one of Harry Bennett's men. Mack had snuck alcohol into a sales meeting at the Dearborn Country Club and proceeded to break up the meeting. Edsel gave Davis the word to fire Harry Mack, confident that he would have his father's support, as the no alcohol policy was Henry Ford's rule.

Harry Bennett had other ideas and convinced Henry that Jack Davis was a liar and that Davis, not Mack, had been responsible for the ruckus at the sales meeting. Henry went to Edsel and ordered him to get Jack Davis out of

his sight. Davis, though not fired, was exiled to the West Coast and demoted to regional sales manager.

Clara Ford, concerned about her son's well-being, went to Charles Sorensen at the Rouge. She broke down in tears, sobbing 'Who is this man Bennett who has so much control over my husband and is ruining my son's health?' But the labor movement had given Bennett a hold on Henry Ford that neither Sorensen nor Clara could break.

By late 1940, the UAW was prepared to wage its final assault on Ford Motor Company. Workers at the Rouge were openly joining the union. Bennett's Service Department would tear off the workers' union buttons, but that didn't deter the men. They would simply put buttons on other men. On 1 April 1941, Bennett fired eight workers for union activities, but the action rallied the other workers, and in a show of support 1500 men staged a sit-down. When Reuther, the union leader who had been beaten at the Battle of the Overpass, heard about the sit-down he raced down to the plant, and by the time he arrived, the entire

Rouge plant—50,000 workers—had walked out.

Henry and Bennett were prepared to fight the workers, but Edsel, who rushed home from a vacation in Florida, made an impassioned plea for the union, and Henry, much to Bennett's disgust, finally agreed to an election. Henry had deluded himself into believing that his employees were still loyal and was dismayed to discover that only 2.5 percent voted 'no union.'

When it came time to sign the formal contract, Henry refused, declaring 'Close the plant if necessary. Let the union take over if it wishes.' Henry's outburst had been Bennett's handiwork, and Edsel feared that violence would erupt throughout the Rouge. Much to his relief and surprise, Henry did sign the closed-shop contract and agreed to pay his workers wages equal to what the other automakers were paying. Later, Henry confessed to Charles Sorensen that Clara had been responsible for his change of heart, insisting that he sign the contract—which she called a peace agreement—to avoid unnecessary bloodshed.

In 1938, Edsel Ford asked the styling department at Lincoln to build him a car based on the Lincoln Zephyr. Following Edsel's directive to make the car 'as continental as possible,' designer Bob Gregorie developed an elegant automobile with a stretched Zephyr hood and various Zephyr trim items. This car (below) became the prototype for the Lincoln Continental.

Far left and overleaf: Though the Lincoln Continental was based on Zephyr parts, each car was virtually handmade. Architect Frank Lloyd Wright called the Continental the most beautiful car ever made.

THE STRUGGLE TO SURVIVE

Facing page: *Edsel Ford believed the Lincoln Zephyr would help Ford Motor Company recover from the Great Depression. As the low-end Lincoln, the Zephyr was comparable to the Packard and the LaSalle.*

Facing page: *Edsel Ford believed the Lincoln Zephyr would help Ford Motor Company recover from the Great Depression. As the low-end Lincoln, the Zephyr was comparable to the Packard and the LaSalle.*

Although the Zephyr did well immediately after its introduction in 1936, sales in subsequent years failed to live up to the company's expectations and it never sold as well as its rivals.

The problems created by the power play between Harry Bennett and Edsel were reflected in Ford's sales. In 1937, Ford Motor Company made a profit of $7 million on $848 million in sales, while Chrysler made $51 million on $770 million and GM made $196 million on $1.6 billion. The downward slide continued until March 1939, when 75,400 cars were sold that month.

In May 1939, the Ford exhibit at the New York World's Fair was drawing people by the thousands. Located on the fair's highest ground, the exhibit covered almost seven acres. Visitors to the exhibit passed under a 25-foot, stainless steel statue of Mercury. Inside, the nature and character of the Ford Motor Company were illustrated through numerous exhibits, climaxing in 'The Road to Tomorrow,' an elevated highway over which people could drive Fords, Mercurys or Linclon Zephyrs.

From the entrance building visitors passed to the Industrial Building and its numerous exhibits of the various manufacturing processes needed to produce a car. Outside the Industrial Building Ford cars were displayed on a patio. The ambience of the outdoor setting was heightened by afternoon and evening concerts conducted by Ferde Grofe and by a central fountain that expressed in abstract terms the power of the automobile. The Ford exhibit owed its style and grace to Edsel, who set up a temporary residence on Manhasset Bay so that he could personally oversee the event. By August, four months after the fair opened, 4,953,610 people had visited the Ford exhibit, with over one million riding on 'The Road of Tomorrow.'

As 1939 came to a close, Ford had sold a total of 567,320 cars, of which 65,884 were Mercurys and 19,940 Linclons. The Mercury had fared well, considering that it a new car, but even so Ford Motor Company was in third place behind GM and Chrysler.

In 1940, sales climbed to 644,162, reaching 702,656 the following year. Ford Motor Company was still in third place. Sales for the Mercury rose to 81,874 in 1941, giving it a respectable 2.19 percent market share. The Lincoln Zephyr, however, did not live up to its original promise. In 1937, the Zephyr had pushed sales of Lincoln up to 25,243, but then sales for both the Zephyr and the regular Lincoln car declined steadily.

Though Ford had lost its position of prominence in the auto industry, the industry as a whole had reached a milestone in its growth by 1941. In 1941, automobile sales almost equalled that of 1929 (4,596,000 to 4,624,879), and more used cars were in circulation than ever before. Thus, the total number of cars and trucks on the road had risen from 26,502,508 in 1929 to 34,472,000 in 1941.

The automobile itself had undergone numerous improvements. Engines were more powerful. The 1925 car that was able to cruise at only 30 mph was capable of 50 mph in 1941. The previous decade had seen the arrival of hydraulic brakes, better transmissions, springs and, in general, a smoother ride. Cars now featured sealed-beam headlights and controlled ventilation.

Improvements in the American road system went hand in hand with advances in the auto industry. In the 1930s, the federal government built 160,000 miles of highway, spending 50 percent more money on road building than it had in the 1920s. At the same time, the states were also busy building up their highway systems, from 315,000 miles to 560,000.

Safety on the road became a primary concern. In addition to distances and destinations, signs warned the motorist of bad curves and intersections. White lanes marked the center of the road and the states required drivers to use hand signals. (Unfortunately, the states did not agree on the same signals, but that would change in time.)

As a consequence of improved road and auto conditions, extended road trips became more common, and the traveler could now find

maps and information on traffic laws, points of interest and places to stay overnight.

The auto had thus reached maturity by 1940. The industry had emerged from the lean years of the Depression stronger and more responsive to the public's needs and desires. Cars were affordable to the average consumer. The 1940 Ford sold for $600, and medium-priced cars, such as the DeSoto and the Packard, sold for roughly $780.

Ford may have been the number three automaker, but it still held an important place in the industry. Millions of people were loyal to Ford and would never drive anything but a Ford. Being part of the Ford team, whether in engineering, manufacturing or sales, carried a mark of distinction. And Henry Ford himself still represented American creativity.

WILLOW RUN

With the United States' entry into World War II, Ford Motor Company became the country's third largest defense contractor, behind General Motors and Curtiss-Wright, the Wright Brothers' plane-making company. Ford produced jeeps, armored cars, troop carriers, trucks, tanks, tank destroyers, Pratt & Whitney aircraft engines and gliders, but the company's biggest contribution to the war effort was the Willow Run project.

Named for a willow-lined stream that ran through Henry Ford's farmland near Ann Arbor, Willow Run was the largest single industrial structure in the world under one roof. In theory, it was designed to roll out B-24 Liberator bombers at the incredible rate of one per

hour. The US Army Air Force was concerned that Consolidated Aircraft, the B-24's designer, would not be able to produce the aircraft in sufficient quantities and approached Ford with the project.

Henry Ford, now almost 80, was amenable to the project, but after suffering two strokes was not physically able to take charge as he had in the past. The project belonged to Edsel and Charles Sorensen, who was invigorated by the challenge of designing the world's first integrated aircraft assembly line. Though Henry Ford was not running the show, he made it all seem possible and that was what the country needed. Willow Run fortified the spirit of the American people. After Pearl Harbor, the country needed to believe that they would triumph in the end. Willow Run became a symbol of that hope. Charles Lindbergh called it 'a sort of Grand Canyon of a mechanized world.' GM produced three times as much material for the war effort as Ford did, but Ford had captured the fancy of the American public.

Reality, however, did not live up to the public's expectations. During World War I, the transition from mass producing cars to mass producing boats was much longer and more difficult than anticipated. Ford now found itself in a similar situation with manufacturing planes. By the end of 1942, Ford had produced only 56 planes, which amounted to only three days' work at the highly touted rate of a plane an hour. Willow Run was suddenly known as 'Willit Run?'

President Franklin D Roosevelt visited the plant in September 1942, and while he conceded that the factory was not yet operational, within a year Willow Run was living up to its promise, eventually exceeding the goal of one plane an hour.

When Roosevelt arrived, Henry was noticeably absent from the welcoming committee and a search party was sent out to discover his whereabouts. He was found off in a corner of the factory experimenting with a new machine. Henry's health had failed considerably since the second stroke. He moved and spoke more slowly and was troubled by lapses of memory. It began to look as if Henry would finally have to pass on the reins of power, but Edsel's health was also poor and Harry Bennett was eager to step into Henry's place.

Even though Bennett was not taken seriously as an executive, he did have an incredible amount of power in the company. His office was essentially the communication hub that transmitted messages to and from all company cars. Through his Service Department, which most people regarded as a network of spies, Bennett knew everything that went on. He knew when someone was hired, fired or transferred. His reach extended across the ocean, for he controlled all travel vouchers.

Left: During World War II, Ford Motor Company became the third largest defense contractor in the nation. Car production ceased and Ford turned its energies to producing jeeps, armored cars, troop carriers, trucks, tanks and airplanes for the war effort.

In the past, Bennett had avoided open confrontations with Edsel, preferring to go behind Edsel's back to Henry. Beneath his surface politeness to Edsel was a layer of contempt. Now he openly referred to Edsel as 'the weakling.' In October 1942, the two men had a serious confrontation, with Bennett once again using his position as head of security to get to Edsel. Bennett told Edsel he planned to encircle the grounds of his home, as well as those of Edsel's two eldest sons, Henry II and Benson, with men from the Service Department. Furious, Edsel told Bennett to stay away from his boys. In the ensuing argument, Edsel accused Bennett of concocting the kidnap stories for Henry's benefit. Bennett was livid and would have struck Edsel had Charles Sorensen not intervened.

The following April, Edsel and Bennett clashed again, this time concerning AW Wibel. Wibel, one of the company's finest employees, had been with Ford since 1912, when he started as a machinist, and had worked his way up to vice president and director in charge of company purchasing. While Edsel was vacationing in Florida, Bennett fired Wibel for refusing to do business with a crony of his. As soon as he returned from Florida, Edsel went

Right: *When the United States became embroiled in World War II, Ford Motor Company began building B-24 bombers at its massive Willow Run facility. By the war's end, over 8000 B-24 Liberators had been assembled by Ford Motor Company.*

Below: *B-24s in action during World War II.*

straight to his father about Wibel's dismissal, but Henry, as usual, stood by Bennett.

Shortly after the Wibel incident, Henry asked Sorensen to talk with Edsel, who by this time was seriously ill, and change his attitude about Bennett. When Sorensen met with Edsel the next morning, Edsel's immediate reaction was to resign. Sorensen persuaded Edsel to stay on, declaring that he too would resign if Edsel left. Later that day Sorensen spoke bluntly with Henry about Edsel and the Wibel situation and then left for Miami, believing that things had been smoothed over, at least for the time being.

While Sorensen headed for Florida, Edsel went to the hospital. For the last several years, he had been plagued by stomach problems. He had undergone an operation for stomach

ulcers in January 1942 and later that year had suffered a severe attack of undulant fever caused by drinking unpasteurized milk from the Ford farm. The reality was that Edsel was dying from stomach cancer. By this time the cancer had spread to his liver, and there was nothing the doctors could do. They sent him home to die. Henry refused to believe that his son was dying and insisted that the doctors at Ford Hospital must be able to make Edsel well.

But Henry Ford was wrong. Edsel Ford died eight days later, on 26 May 1943 at the age of 49.

With Edsel's death, Ford Motor Company was left without a president. Harry Bennett and Charles Sorensen both viewed themselves as viable candidates for the position, but the day before Edsel's funeral, Henry Ford shocked everyone by announcing that he would resume

the presidency—the position he had retired from almost a quarter of a century earlier.

Bennett was concerned that Sorensen was plotting a takeover and rushed out to Willow Run to assess the situation. Sorensen was too preoccupied with keeping the plant running to mastermind a takeover plot. A month later, Bennett appointed himself Sorensen's assistant. Washington was concerned that without Edsel to manage the situation, Ford would not be able to fulfill its contractual obligations and sent Ernest Kanzler, now working as director general for the Office of War Production, to Detroit. Kanzler suggested that Henry II be relieved of his naval duty and allowed to return to Ford.

Bennett had anticipated a move like this. Under his direction and supposedly at the behest of Henry Ford, Bennett had the company lawyer, IA Capizzi, draw up a codicil to Henry's will establishing a trust that would control Ford Motor Company for 10 years after Henry's death. None of Henry Ford's grandchildren were included in the board of trustees; Bennett, however, was the secretary of the trust.

The Ford family knew nothing of this codicil, but the women of the family were nonetheless prepared to take a stand regarding the management of the company. Eleanor Clay Ford had watched Edsel's suffering and knew the part that Bennett had played in it. Clara, too, believed Bennett had caused her son much pain. Both women wanted Henry Ford II to control Ford Motor Company—if not now, then someday.

HENRY II

L ate in July 1943, Henry Ford II received a brief letter from Navy Secretary Knox: 'You are hereby released from the Navy to get you back to work at the Ford Motor Company.' To most of the people back in Detroit, Henry II seemed far too young and immature to assume such an awesome responsibility.

As a child, young Henry Ford had wanted for nothing. He attended an East Coast prep school, Hotchkiss, which groomed young men from fine families for Ivy League schools. Academically, Henry was far from a shining star, but he did impress his teachers with his sense of humor. Henry went on to Yale, where his academic performance was dismal at times. Legend has it that Henry purchased a term paper on Thomas Hardy from the local term paper mill and left the sales slip inside the paper. His response to this situation reveals a great deal about himself: 'I may be stupid but I'm not that stupid.' Years later, when he made a speech to the Yale Political Union, he opened with the remark, 'I didn't write this one either.'

Just before starting Yale, Henry toured Europe, and on the return trip he met Anne McDonnell, the blond, vivacious daughter of a well-to-do New York stockbroker. The romance blossomed while Henry attended Yale, and by the time he was 21, the two were secretly engaged. Edsel and Eleanor may have felt that their son was a bit young for marriage, but didn't object to the marriage, believing that marriage might settle him down. Old Henry, however, took a dim view of the situation, for Anne McDonnell was Catholic and young Henry planned to convert to Catholicism.

When Henry and Anne returned from their honeymoon in Hawaii, their wedding present from Edsel and Eleanor was waiting for them: a Georgian home in Grosse Pointe and 25,000 shares of Ford Motor Company stock, as Edsel explained, 'in recognition of the fact that you are finishing your college career this month

and after being married will join the Ford Motor Company as your future business....'

As it had been for Edsel, Ford Motor Company was his destiny. Henry II, along with his brother Benson, had worked at the Rouge before he enlisted, and it was understood that he would return to Ford as soon as the war was over. When Henry II returned to the Rouge on 10 August 1943, he appreciated the struggle that lay before him. Henry II spent his first few weeks at Ford poring over his father's files. Then he traveled around the country, reassuring dealers that Ford would stay in business, but when he looked around the Rouge, Henry saw mismanagement and confusion. Manufacturing had too many workers, while engineering desperately needed new men with fresh ideas. There was no schedule for ordering materials, nor was there a system for making and checking plans. Financial statements were carefully guarded.

Henry II was savvy enough to be wary of Bennett and expected his grandfather to treat him somewhat suspiciously. Henry II had decided to move into his father's office in the engineering lab. His grandfather ordered the office locked, so Henry II moved into Edsel's old office at the Administration Building, knowing that his grandfather avoided the place because it was too full of painful memories.

Henry Ford was deteriorating rapidly, both mentally and physically, and his grandson took great care not to say or do anything that might disturb him. Henry did what he could to shield his grandfather from the press, telling them that Henry was in excellent health and putting a lot of effort into the Willow Run plant. With Old Henry quickly fading, the uneasy truce that had existed between Bennett and Sorensen was dissolving.

Harry Bennett did not consider Henry II as a threat, but he nevertheless sought to neutralize whatever threat existed by offering assistance to the young man. Both men adapted a

Facing page: Henry Ford II (seen here in the 1970s) was released from the Navy in 1943 to help his grandfather, who was now in his eighties, run Ford Motor Company. Under the guidance of Henry II, the financially struggling company was reorganized, eventually regaining its position of dominance in the auto industry.

Previous pages: After three years of producing war materials, Ford, and the rest of the Detroit automakers, returned to manufacturing cars with the 1946 model year. This is a 1946 Mercury station wagon.

false air of affability. Benson was outraged at his brother's hypocrisy and refused to have anything to do with the man who had caused their father so much heartache, but Henry was a realist and preferred to handle Bennett his way, realizing that Bennett could not be trusted. Bennett had a habit of disappearing, supposedly to confer with Old Henry. He would report back that 'Mr Ford wants us to do it this way.' Henry prudently checked on Bennett and discovered, as he had expected, that Bennett had never conferred with Mr Ford.

In his struggle to gain control, Bennett conducted a purge of upper management. He dismissed the public relations counsel hired by Edsel, replacing him with one of his own men, John W Thompson. John Crawford, a close associate of Edsel's and a man known for his integrity and vision, was pressured into leaving. Likewise, Fred Black, who had successfully handled the company's exhibits at foreign expositions, was ousted.

One of Ford's most serious losses was Laurence Sheldrick. Recognized as one of the industry's finest engineers, Sheldrick, along with Edsel, had worked on a design for the postwar conditions—a small economy car. Sheldrick was also working on such things as independent suspension and four-wheel drive. Soon after his arrival at the Rouge, Henry II talked with Sheldrick about the postwar designs. They also discussed meeting with federal ordnance officers with whom the company was doing business. Charles Sorensen disapproved of their discussion and told Sheldrick so in no uncertain terms. The ensuing argument ended with Sheldrick's resignation. In retrospect, Sheldrick concluded that Old Henry and Bennett had manipulated Sorensen into starting the fight that led to his departure.

Sorensen was well aware that Ford Motor Company was hurting itself with the departure of some of its finest men, but he was powerless to do anything about it and, in fact, would soon be in the same situation himself. By mid-1943, he was overworked and under considerable stress from dealing with the production problems at Willow Run.

Finally, in November of 1943, Charles Sorensen told Henry Ford that he wished to be 'released' effective 1 January 1944. He advised Henry that Washington was concerned about the loss of key personnel and the effect it would have on the Willow Run bomber project. Sorensen added that Henry II should be appointed president immediately. Sorensen apparently made some headway with the elder Ford because Henry II was elected vice president on 15 December.

Sorensen left for Florida around New Year's Day. He had not officially resigned and kept requesting his release. Henry finally replied on 4 March 1944 by asking for Sorensen's resignation, citing Sorensen's aspiration to wrest control from him. Sorensen—outraged, and justifiably so—resigned. With the war still raging, Sorensen's dismissal made the federal government doubly worried about Willow Run, and it even considered removing Henry Ford and putting the project in the hands of the War Board. Sorensen objected to this, and assured Washington that Henry II could handle the situation.

With Sorensen removed, Bennett had only Henry II blocking his path to power. Bennett was in a strong position. He had placed numerous cronies in high positions; he had his network of secret police; he dominated the failing Henry Ford; and most of all he had the codicil that created the Trust.

Henry II, however, was in a potentially stronger psition for a number of reasons. First, his election as vice president accorded him authority among the lower ranks. Second, Washington depended on him to handle Willow Run, and once he proved that he could, the War Board supported Henry II completely. Third, his family was behind him. Both Clara Ford and Eleanor were adamantly opposed to Bennett. The two women were strong-minded, particularly when it came to protecting family, and they controlled a substantial block of voting stock. Henry II's brothers, Benson and William, were equally supportive.

In addition, Henry II would prove that he had the talent and skills needed to be an effective leader. As Henry perceived the situation, he had three interrelated goals: establish correct policies; remove the malignancies from administration; and hire honest, reliable assistants. His first step was to surround himself with capable assistants: Mead Bricker, Logan Miller, John S Bugas and John Davis. Bricker and Miller were seasoned hands at Ford, while Bugas was a former FBI agent hired by Bennett to deal with labor relations. Much to Bennett's dismay, Bugas had immediately become a supporter of Henry II. John Davis was the sales manager who had been demoted to the West Coast following the Edsel-Bennett confrontation about Harry Mack. At first, Davis was reluctant to return to Dearborn and a possible showdown with his old nemesis, but Henry II assured him they would fight their battles together.

Shortly after Henry II had gathered this small

army, he learned of the codicil. His immediate reaction was to resign, sell his stock and urge all the Ford dealers to break their connection with the company. Bugas calmed him down and went to discuss the matter with Harry Bennett. Bennett was greatly perturbed but agreed to 'straighten the whole thing out' the next day, adding that Henry II didn't need to be bothered and the two of them could deal with the matter.

The next day Bennett remained uncharacteristically calm. He showed Bugas the codicil and a carbon copy of it and then, with a dramatic flourish, lit a match. When the codicil was reduced to ashes, he swept them into an envelope for Bugas to present to Henry. The motivation behind Bennett's performance is difficult to discern, but Capizzi, the attorney who drew up the document, speculated that Henry Ford had never signed it.

Whether or not the codicil was ever valid is a moot point, for its discovery alone was enough to rally Henry II, his family and his associates into action with an urgency that had not existed previously. On 10 April 1944, Henry II managed to have himself appointed executive vice president. As second-in-command, Henry II now had authority, at least in theory, over Bennett. Henry II and his four aides spent the summer and fall of 1944 planning the best course of action. The men met at the Detroit Club so their sessions would escape the eyes and ears of Bennett's men. In July, Henry and John Davis toured New England giving pep talks to all the dealers. The war would soon be ending and Ford would be putting all its energy back into producing passenger cars. Henry II was able to reassure the dealers that the new models would be successful.

While Henry II was diligently working to assume control of the company, his grandmother Clara was pursuing the same cause in her own way. She was determined that Bennett would not take control of Ford Motor Company. To that end, she instructed the operator at Fair Lane to always tell Bennett that Mr Ford was not at home. It was time for Henry to step down and appoint Henry II in his place, and Clara finally persuaded Henry to do just that. On 20 September 1945, Henry Ford summoned his grandson to Fair Lane to tell him he was handing the presidency over to him. Henry accepted—on the condition that he have a free hand to make any changes he wished. The two Henrys argued about that for a time but, as Henry later recalled, 'he didn't withdraw the offer.'

The next day a board meeting was held to make it all official. Harry Bennett started to leave the room when Henry's resignation letter was read, but the others prevailed on him to stay through the election.

Henry Ford II's first act as president was to fire Harry Bennett.

Opposite page: An advertisement proclaiming the universal appeal of the 1947 Ford. In the booming postwar seller's market, Ford output exceeded 600,000 for 1947.

THE ROAD TO RECOVERY

After the end of World War II, Henry Ford II quickly moved the company back into car production. Between September and December 1945, Ford was once again the industry leader, producing 34,439 cars.

The 1946 Fords used prewar bodies, with some styling and mechanical changes. Fords for 1947 were little changed from the 1946 models, with only such minor alterations as lower-mounted parking lights. A 1947 Super Deluxe coupe is seen on the facing page.

Henry II had won his first battle by ousting Harry Bennett, but the company that he now controlled was plagued by numerous ills. As John Davis saw it, 'When young Henry came here the company was not only dying, it was already dead, and *rigor mortis* was setting in.'

Though Davis' statement is a bit extreme, Ford Motor Company was beset with considerable problems. The struggle for power had left a trail of resignations and dismissals, weakening a hierarchy of control that was tenuous to begin with. Uncertainty was the byword of the day. When Henry II looked around him, he saw gross inefficiency, later estimating that workers were functioning at a third of their normal rate.

The end of the war created a set of problems as the company prepared to convert to peacetime production. Factories needed to be remodeled and retooled and new plants built. Prior to the war, Ford had fallen to third place behind Chevrolet and Chrysler, and to rebound Ford would need brilliant new designs, yet the engineering staff was seriously handicapped. It was the challenge of developing Ford's first postwar car to which Henry II now turned.

On 25 May 1945, the War Production Board gave the auto industry permission to manufacture 200,000 cars, of which Ford was allotted 39,910 units. By 2 June, Ford unveiled 'a hand-made model.' The new car was an updated version of a 1942 model, with a 100 hp engine instead of 90 hp. It featured better springs and brakes and assorted cosmetic changes. Ford was the first carmaker to display its new car to the eager public, prompting the *Kansas City Times* to comment 'It is just like Henry Ford to be the first under the wire.'

On 14 August 1945, the Japanese surrendered and the government lifted the restrictions it had placed on raw materials, freeing the carmakers to produce an unlimited number of cars. Ford planned to manufacture more than

twice as many cars as it had originally been allotted.

Henry II's optimistic goals suffered a setback a few days later when the Kelsey-Hayes Wheel Company went on strike. Without wheels, there could be no cars; consequently, Ford Motor Company was forced to lay off 75,000 workers. The Kelsey-Hayes strike ended on 8 October, but only three days later, 1000 millwrights walked off their jobs, and the Aluminum Company of America went on strike. Then, on 20 November, Kelsey-Hayes stopped all deliveries. Ford continued to be plagued by their suppliers' strikes and stoppages.

In spite of these difficulties, Ford unveiled the new 1946 car on 26 October—'V8 Day'—and by the next day, 300,000 customers ordered the car even though the price had not been set. The Office of Price Administration (OPA), a government agency, regulated pricing of automobiles and the parts that went into manufacturing them, and, in an effort to stave off inflation, set prices at the 1942 level. As a result of the OPA regulations and the various work stoppages by its suppliers, Ford was losing $300 a car.

Henry Ford II responded to the OPA in a straightforward manner, stating that Ford Motor Company would continue to produce cars at as high a volume as possible and that the company would attempt to improve its efficiency. In spite of these measures, Henry Ford II believed that Ford Motor Company would lose a substantial amount of money in 1946.

Chester Bowles, the head of the OPA, was outraged by Ford's comments, stating that Henry Ford II was undermining the work of the OPA. Bowles believed that low production was not the fault of the OPA, but as Henry II explained, 'Shortages on only a few parts can stop the whole assembly line.' Eventually, President Truman allowed Ford Motor Company to increase its prices. Although the change came too late to turn around Ford's economic woes, the controversy with the OPA showed that young Henry Ford had the makings of an effective leader, not only for his own company but also for the automotive industry as a whole.

Henry also made the auto industry take notice with his speech to the Society of Automotive Engineers at their annual meeting in Detroit in January 1946. The speech, entitled 'The Challenge of Human Engineering,' marked Henry Ford II's first public appearance as the head of Ford Motor Company. Labor relations within the automotive industry had been strained for some time and Henry addressed the situation head on, calling for a better relationship between management and labor. 'There is no reason why a grievance case should not be handled with the same dispatch as a claim for insurance benefits,' he declared. 'There is no reason why a contract could not be written and agreed upon with the same efficiency and good temper that marks the negotiation of a commercial contract between two companies.' For 1946, the concept that management had responsibilities toward its employees was radical.

The response to Henry's speech was immediate. He received front page coverage in all the major American newspapers, with words such as *courage*, *candor* and *statesmanship* describing him. Overnight, Henry became a figure of national stature and within a month his picture graced the cover of *Time* magazine.

Henry's philosophy of 'human engineering' would guide him throughout his tenure as the leader of Ford Motor Company. Years after the

speech, in the late 1970s, UAW leader Douglas Fraser remarked, 'We knew that Ford policy was ultimately and decisively controlled by a man who was willing to break new ground and who was sensitive to human considerations.'

THE WHIZ KIDS

Henry II's next move was a daring one. The company was losing $1 million dollars a day and had not made a profit in 15 years. In an effort to revitalize the company, Henry hired a group of 10 former air force officers who became known as the Whiz Kids.

After the war, the officers decided they could market themselves as a management team using the planning and financial skills they had developed in the air force. The men had served together in the Office of Statistical Control, the administrative branch of the US Army Air Force. In short, the OSC got the air force where it needed to be. It was no easy task to arrange for the proper number of men and planes and the right amount of fuel,

Below: *Whereas a Ford was a car for everyone (see the advertisement on page 83), a Mercury was the car for the 'young modern.'*

Edsel Ford had pioneered Ford's Mercury Division in the late 1930s as a counterpart to GM's mid-priced Buick and Pontiac divisions.

ammunition and so on to arrive at one place at one time. By the war's end, the 10 young officers had acquired skills in cost analysis, price control and management.

Charles Bates 'Tex' Thornton, one of the youngest colonels in the air force, was known as Young Napoleon. As the war wound down he turned his talents to the private sector and organized the group, which consisted of Robert S McNamara, Charles Bosworth, Arjay R Miller, Ben D Mills, George Moore, James O Wright, Wilbur Anderson, Francis C 'Jack' Reith and J Edward Lundy. Ranging in age from 26 to 34, the men had considerable business expertise in peacetime as well. McNamara had been on the faculty of the Harvard Business School, while Lundy had been at Princeton. The others' experience included positions with the federal government or in law. Thornton sent Henry Ford II a telegram that read, in part: 'We would like to discuss with you personally a matter of management importance and request early meeting.' Ford responded by inviting the group to Detroit.

Prior to the group's arrival, Ernest Kanzler arranged for Henry II to speak with Robert Lovett, the Under-Secretary of War, who recommended the men wholeheartedly. Henry liked the group immediately. They were of the same age as he was, and shared Henry's views on the role of business in the postwar economy. They knew nothing of cars, but they had known nothing about planes before they revolutionized the Air Force. The Whiz Kids were equally impressed with Henry Ford II.

The team was scheduled to start at Ford on 1 February 1946. They arrived a day earlier. The one-month orientation turned into four months, and then the men began going around to various departments, asking questions and scribbling answers on pads. Because they asked so many questions, people started calling them the Quiz Kids. Someone else dubbed them the Whiz Kids, and the name stuck.

In the accounting department, Arjay Miller discovered that the bookkeepers kept piles of bills up to four feet high and estimated accounts payable by measuring the stack. Employees were paid in cash because Old Henry had long ago discovered that the men cashed their checks in saloons, and Henry disapproved of drinking. When the company's controller was asked what he estimated some figures would be in six months, his reply was 'What would you like them to be?'

The Whiz Kids would leave a mark on Ford Motor Company. In time, from their ranks would come two presidents and six vice presidents. But in 1946, they were young and inexperienced and Henry II needed help now. He found it in Ernest R Breech.

Ernie Breech was a self-made man from Lebanon, Missouri, a small town in the Ozark

Mountains. The son of a blacksmith, Ernie grew up reading the books of Horatio Alger and took the stories to heart. While in high school, he earned money trapping rabbits. He supported himself in college by ironing other students' clothes and selling Victrolas door to door.

After college, he worked as a bookkeeper and soon earned his CPA. Breech worked as a controller for several companies, finally ending up at GM as Alfred Sloan's chief problem solver. He was appointed president of Bendix Aviation, a GM subsidiary, and it was assumed that he would move into the top spot at GM, but internal relations within GM worked against him.

Henry Ford II met with Ernie Breech, outlining the plans he had for revitalizing Ford, but Breech was reluctant to join the Ford team. Undaunted, Henry II convinced him to come take a look at things and offer some advice. Breech discovered that the company was, in his own words, 'really a mess.' The challenge of solving such a mess was compelling. Moreover, Breech felt a kinship to Henry II. His own son was just a year younger than Henry, and he wondered if his son was in a bind, would there be someone to help him? Breech agreed to take the job, beginning 1 July 1946.

Breech knew he would need help reorganizing Ford and immediately began recruiting top personnel from GM. The finance and engineering departments at Ford Motor Company were among the most troubled, so Breech naturally sought experts in those areas. Breech hired Lewis D Crusoe to head the finance department. When he started at Ford, Crusoe was 52 and living in semiretirement at his ranch in Cheboygan, Michigan. Crusoe had earned his degree by attending night school at the

Above: *A 1948 Lincoln Continental convertible. Sales of the exclusive Lincoln Continental did well in the late 1940s, in spite of postwar inflation. Production rose from 466 cars in 1946 to 1569 cars in 1947, even as the price for a Continental coupe went from $4392 to $4662.*

Above: *A 1948 Ford Super Deluxe coupe.*

Far right: *After the war, Ford lured buyers back into the showroom by dressing up a convertible in a rich wood trim. The Sportsman convertible sold for $500 more than a conventional all-steel convertible and was produced in relatively small numbers: 1209 in 1946, 2250 in 1947 and only 28 in 1948.*

Though rare, the Sportsman served its purpose admirably: It made something ordinary special and increased the traffic in dealerships. Today an automotive classic, the Sportsman is a noteworthy example of Ford's ingenuity in the postwar years.

University of Detroit. He demanded accuracy but he also inspired those who worked for him. As one of his assistants later remarked, 'He inspired great loyalty because, unlike so many executives, he wasn't just pushing himself forward. When you worked for him, you were *making* cars.'

Breech made Crusoe his executive assistant and put him in charge of Tex Thornton's Whiz Kids. The men were shocked by the condition of the company's financial records. There was no certified balance sheet nor property records. One bank account drew absolutely no interest. By the end of 1946, the team had arrived at a projected balance, but as finances had been in such disarray, they doubted their own figures and brought in an accounting firm.

To battle the problems in engineering, Breech brought on Harold T Youngren, formerly with Oldsmobile and presently the chief engineer at Borg-Warner. Youngren was dissatisfied with Borg-Warner because he believed he spent too much of his time being an executive and not enough time as an engineer.

Even though Breech had surrounded himself with able men, at times the task seemed almost insurmountable. The engineering department was outdated; the dealer organization was chaotic; the upper echelons of management had been purged during the Bennett power struggle; employee theft was

rampant; and the company owed a $50 million tax surcharge for excess profits at Willow Run. Breech was depressed about the situation, and for the first time in his life felt overwhelmed. Then he recalled an old adage from his childhood about breaking an unmanageable bundle of sticks: break one at a time.

THE 1949 FORD

One of the first 'sticks' that Breech confronted was the 1949 Ford. When he first arrived at Ford, Breech sat through numerous product-planning sessions. All the designs were dressed up versions of the 1946 car, which itself was a remake of the 1942. Mechanically, the car belonged in the 1930s. The V8 engine still had cooling problems. While GM was busy working on automatic transmissions and front-end suspensions, Ford's engineering department was doing almost nothing. At a planning meeting, Breech suggested a totally renovated car, but was told it would take three years to complete. As he drove home that night, Breech pondered the question and said a prayer for guidance. The next day he announced to the policy committee, 'We start from scratch.'

The 1949 Ford was the first absolutely new, popularly priced car since the end of the war. The car was low and light, with a smooth, aerodynamic styling. The mechanical specifications were almost completely new and included overdrive, available as an option.

The 1949 Ford was only the fourth major automobile—after the Model T, Model A, and V8—in the history of the company. The cost of retooling the factory amounted to $72 million, but the gamble paid off. Sales in 1949, including Mercurys and Lincolns, passed the million mark for the first time since 1930. Ford was still in third place, but growing stronger.

The public liked the new Ford and so did old Henry Ford himself. Early in 1947, Henry and Clara visited the laboratory to view the first full-size clay model of the new car. The model was so realistic that Clara pulled the clay handle off when she attempted to open the door. Henry questioned the engineers about the type of engine that would go into the car. Both an eight-cylinder and six-cylinder were planned, and those who knew of Henry's dislike of the six-cylinder waited with some trepidation for his reaction to the six-cylinder. Henry calmly left the room. The changing of the guard had already taken place.

Henry's health was failing fast, and he and Clara decided to spend the duration of winter in the warmth of Georgia. When they returned in April, Henry's condition had improved and on the morning of 7 April 1947, he seemed like his old self. Heavy rains had plunged the powerplant at Fair Lane underwater, leaving the estate without electricity or telephones. The

electricity came on long enough for Henry to listen to his favorite radio show, but soon went out again. A few hours after Henry and Clara had gone to bed, the doctor was summoned to the house. When he reached Fair Lane about midnight, Henry Ford was already dead, having left the world just as he entered it—by candlelight.

The nation and the world paid homage to Henry Ford. The man who invented the Model T was eulogized by President Harry Truman, Winston Churchill, Joseph Stalin and other world leaders. Over 100,000 people paid their respects while his body lay in state at the Henry Ford Museum.

When Henry Ford left the farm as a young man, one in five people lived in the city. By the time of his death, the figures were reversed, and Henry Ford's Model T was, in part, behind the change. The public's demand for Henry's Tin Lizzie inspired Highland Park, the finest factory in the world, and led to the development of mass production, a process that altered the industrial world. With the institution of the $5.00 a day wage, Henry Ford forged the notion that a worker should be paid a decent wage for a day's work. A shrewd businessman, he was also an idealist, as evidenced by the Peace Ship, his support of schools, his study of food and nutrition, and his desire to bring history to the people through his museum and Greenfield Village. He was an American hero.

Above: *Born into the world of horse-drawn carriages, Henry Ford, more than any other individual, represented the auto industry. Ford died at his Fair Lane estate on 7 April 1947.*

Overleaf: *A 1949 Custom convertible. The 1949 Fords were the first all-new postwar models. Retooling costs were tremendous, but the effort paid off.*

FORD AROUND THE WORLD

When Henry Ford II was handed the difficult job of rebuilding Ford Motor Company, one of the many tasks that confronted him was revitalizing the company's international operations. Both at home and abroad, Ford Motor Company was in wretched condition.

Ford's European plants had continued operations during World War II, primarily building tractors. Henry Ford made his first tour of the European plants in 1948. In Germany, operations at Ford-Werke in Cologne were running as best they could under the circumstances, but the workers' morale was extremely low. In a few short years, a new factory would be built for the Taunus, a collaborative effort between design teams in Germany and Dearborn. The first Taunus rolled off the assembly line in 1952, and by the following year 50,000 cars had been built in order to keep up with the demand. When Henry Ford returned to Germany in 1954, he found a thriving company and optimistic managers.

In France, the plant at Poissy reflected the state of the country. France was deep in debt and still suffering from the antagonism between the resistance movement and the Vichy collaborators. Henry Ford was able to supply the French operations with some funds, but not enough to bail it out completely. Ford of France ended up borrowing nine million dollars from banks. The next year, the company's president resigned, and the banks selected his replacement: Francois Lehideux, a former department store manager, whose closest connection to the automobile was his wife's family name—Renault.

By 1952 Ford of France was in even worse shape and Henry Ford and Ernest Breech met with the French bankers to propose a solution to this dreadful state of affairs. Lehideux would remain with the company, but the actual management would be handled by an American. The man chosen for the task was Jack Reith, one of the Whiz Kids.

Ford of France had always been overshadowed by the country's own carmakers—Citroen, Peugeot and Renault. After the war, Dearborn decided that Ford of France could better compete with the three native carmakers by offering a larger car—the Vedette. The Vedette had failed to ignite the enthusiasm of the French public and had in fact contributed to leading the company to the edge of bankruptcy.

Reith not only improved the Vedette, but soon had Ford of France operating at a profit. He realized that Ford Motor Company would be better off financially by importing cars from England and Germany to France rather than building them in France, so he proposed a merger with the Simca Car Company (Société Industrielle de Méchanique et Carrosserie) in which Ford received 15.2 percent of Simca stock. Henry Ford set up a new company to market Ford products in France and later sold his interest in Simca to Chrysler at a profit.

Jack Reith had accomplished a task that would have stymied most. France awarded him the Legion and Honor and asked him to

this

stay in France and work his magic with Simca. Instead, Reith returned to Dearborn, where he was assigned the responsibility of supervising the Edsel project. Unfortunately for Reith, his name became associated with a project that failed rather than with one that succeeded.

Meanwhile, Ford of England was doing well in spite of itself. Ford Motor Company had had plants in England since 1904, when Henry Ford I had reached an agreement with his friend, Baron Percival Lea Dewhurst Perry. That agreement gave the British company controlling interests in the Ford companies of Italy, Egypt, Spain, Holland and Denmark, as well as the right to sell Fords all over Europe.

Products were not a problem for Ford of England. During the postwar years, Ford was the leading automaker in England, producing the Anglia, the Prefect and the Popular, which lived up to its name. In later years, Ford of England produced the Consul, the Zephyr and the Cortina—another big seller. The company also manufactured a highly successful diesel tractor.

The problem lay in the organization. There was no coordination among the various Ford companies in Europe. With conditions the way they were, the British would have been more than happy to relinquish their controlling interests in the other companies, but strict governmental regulations made that impossible. Finally, under a complex procedure known as the scheme of arrangement, Ford of England declared a large dividend of seven million pounds. Because Ford Motor Company could not take the cash out of the country, it gave the dividend back to Ford of England in exchange for its share in the other European companies.

The stock trade gave Ford Motor Company the control that it needed to straighten things out. In Italy, the governmental restrictions made it difficult to compete with Fiat, so the plant there was reduced to a distribution center. The company pulled out of Spain completely.

In 1967, Ford consolidated its various European operations into one group, Ford of Europe. The consolidation smoothed the way for the Taunus-Transit, a medium-sized van that John Andrews, the head of Ford Germany, believed he could sell in both Germany and England. Later, the British Ford Cortina was sold as a German car. Then, in 1976, Ford of Europe developed its finest product yet—the Fiesta, a car designed to meet the requirements of every European market.

Ford of Europe helped make Ford Motor Company the most profitable European manufacturing company of the post-World War II era. When Ford in the United States was struggling through the energy crisis, Ford of Europe remained profitable, and in fact kept Ford Motor Company from the brink of financial disaster. Ford of Europe also proved to be a

training ground for rising young executives at Ford, and when the company was in the doldrums that affected all of Detroit in the 1970s, the managers who had worked in Europe provided the inspiration for cars with European styling and engineering.

FORD OF CANADA

Ford of Canada had been around almost as long as Ford itself. Established on 17 August 1904, just one year after the parent company, Ford of Canada had always maintained close ties to the parent company. Separated from Ford by only the Detroit River, Ford of Canada produced basically the same cars as the parent company, and was in fact dependent on Dearborn for designing, styling and engineering. In 1950, however, it lost the top spot to General Motors and, under the guidance of President RM Sales, instituted major changes. The headquarters were moved from Windsor to Oakville, near Toronto, and the Windsor facilities were converted to an engine factory and machine shop.

A few of the cars produced by Ford of England during the 1950s and early 1960s: the Consul sedan (at top), the squire wagon (above) and the Popular coupe (far left).

Ford of Canada owned subsidiaries in India, Australia, New Zealand, Malaysia, Rhodesia and South Africa. Throughout the 1950s, sales in these countries continued to increase, except in India. In 1950, the Indian government prohibited the importation of finished automobiles. Ford of Canada's response was to consolidate its Indian branches, but in 1954, as governmental restrictions increased, Ford of Canada placed Ford of India in voluntary liquidation.

Meanwhile, Ford of Canada's Australian subsidiary began to do more and more of its own manufacturing.

FORD AUSTRALIA

Since the days of the Model T, Ford had been a major force in the Australian auto market. In 1938, when it developed the 'coupe utility,' Ford showed it had the ability to respond to the unique needs of rural Australia. Years later, the success of this project led Ford Motor Company to allow Ford Australia to modify the Falcon design to suit Australia.

The first Australian Falcon was released in 1960. The basic vehicle underwent 13 facelifts in an incredible 28 years of production, before a major redesign in 1988. The original X series chassis was the same as the chassis on the American Falcon, but the XK Falcon was more than just a modified American car. With Ford

Australia's contributions to its design, it was almost a full-bodied Australian car.

Unfortunately, both the XK Falcon and its successor, the XL Falcon, were rife with problems, which persisted until the 1965 XP Falcon. By this time, however, Ford had to prove that the problems had been corrected, so the company staged an eight-day speed and reliability trial over 115,000 kilometers (70,000 miles). The Falcons did well—five finished the event, setting new speed and reliability records—and the car became a best seller. The 1965 XP Falcon won the *Wheels* magazine Car of the Year (COTY) award.

The next year, Ford won the COTY again with the 1966 XR Falcon, which was powered by V8, 4.7-liter (287-ci) engine capable of 201 hp. Supply of this popular car could not keep up with demand.

Like the XR Falcon, the Australian-designed ZA Fairlane was an immediate success. Equipped with either an in-line six or a V8, the Fairlane was essentially a luxury Falcon with a longer wheelbase.

By the early 1970s, Ford was challenging Australia's leading carmaker, GM-Holden, for the top spot. In 1974, thanks to the success of the XB Falcon, ZG Fairlane and P5 LTD, Ford was the leader in the passenger market sector for the first time ever.

Ford Australia also did well in the small/medium sector, with the Consul, Zephyr and

Opposite, top: *First produced in Britain, the Mark I Cortina was modified to suit the Australian market and was quickly accepted by the Australian buyer.*

Opposite, bottom: *Also modified for Australia, the TC Cortina Six featured a high torque engine for 'lazy' cruising.*

Above: *Ford Australia's Escort RS2000 was quite popular in the early 1980s.*

Prefect in the 1950s. In the 1960s, Ford introduced the British-derived Cortina, which lasted on the market for 20 years. In the early 1980s, Ford brought out the Laser. The car sold incredibly well and set the standard for the small car market for the rest of the decade. With the Meteor, the sedan version of the Laser, Ford had the market cornered.

ACROSS THE GLOBE

Since the early years of the twentieth century, Ford had been a name with worldwide recognition, and by 1959 the company had assembly plants in Antwerp, Alexandria, Copenhagen, Cork, Brisbane and São Paulo. In addition to the countries mentioned above, Ford owned, or had a controlling interest in, subsidiaries in Sweden, Finland, Argentina, Venezuela, and Portugal, among others.

In 1966, Ford Motor Company and Palestine Automobile Corporation, Ltd made plans to build trucks and tractors in Israel. For 30 years, Palestine Automobile Corporation had been distributing Ford products in Israel. In the early 1960s, sales had increased dramatically, up to 250,000 units. As demand increased, it made sense for Ford to have the cars assembled locally.

The Arab League, however, objected to Ford's plan to do business with the Israelis and threatened to boycott all Ford products, in spite of the fact that there were prosperous Ford dealers in Lebanon, Syria, Jordan, Iraq, Saudi Arabia and the United Arab Republic— all of which had good relationships with the parent company. Ford Motor Company, however, held firm to its position.

Henry Ford said his decision not to yield to the Arab League's demands was 'just pragmatic business procedure.' Those close to Henry Ford add that he was also motivated by a desire to provide economic opportunities for people of all nations.

Opposite, top: *Like its American counterpart, the European Escort is a compact car, but there are some styling differences between the two models.*

Opposite, bottom: *Ford of Europe's Fiesta was one of the best-selling cars in Europe throughout the 1980s.*

Below: *The Sierra Ghia sedan was produced by Ford of England.*

FORD CELEBRATES FIFTY YEARS

As Ford Motor Company headed for its fiftieth anniversary in 1953, the post-war recovery was well on its way. The 1949 Ford was symbolic of the company's recovery. Though still in third place, Ford was less than 5000 cars behind Chrysler. Demand for the 1949 Ford exceeded supply, and everyone wanted to sell the new car. JR Davis, head of sales, was flooded with applications for franchises, with 25 applicants for every opening.

The car was a credit to the organizational and production skills of Breech and his associates, but it also bore the mark of Henry Ford. The car was introduced with a fanfare in the gold and white ballroom of the Waldorf Astoria as champagne flowed and an orchestra serenaded the thousands of people eager to glimpse the elegant new Ford. Advertising featured the car at a country club or parked at a mansion. More than a car for the masses, it belonged to everyone, from the average consumer to the wealthy buyer.

In spite of the promise of the new car, the 1949 Ford was plagued with thousands of minor defects. When Ford executives met to discuss the situation, department heads laid the blame on another department. Breech believed that a specialized division responsible for the defects would facilitate correcting the problems. Breech's vision of a Ford Division had been a dream of his for some time. It would require major reorganization of the company: Assembly, Sales and Advertising, Service Parts and Accessories, and a portion of Purchasing and the Controller's Office were all rolled into the new Ford Division. Lewis Crusoe was named head of the new division.

The company reorganization brought order, and Ford Motor Company began to prosper. The bugs worked out of the 1949 Ford, it was introduced as the 1952 Ford. Sales surpassed those of Chrysler, and Ford slowly gained a foothold against Chevrolet. 'Beat Chevrolet' signs were posted at the end of every assembly line. By 1954 Henry Ford and Ernie Breech were

rewarded with a market share of 30.83 percent, the best since the glory days of the Model T.

The 1950s saw a number of innovations. Beginning in 1951, Ford offered an optional two-speed 'Ford-O-Matic' transmission. In 1954, the company introduced 'the hottest engine in the low-priced field'—an overhead valve four-block V8 capable of producing up to 130 hp. The same year a ball-joint front end suspension was introduced.

The era also produced several innovations in styling, not the least of which were vivid two-tone color schemes and lots of shiny chrome trim. In addition, designer David Ash developed a forerunner of today's sunroof with his transparent plastic roof section for the Crestline Skyliner. In 1957, car buyers were given the option of a hardtop convertible. A complicated mechanism lowered the roof into the trunk of the car. Ford sold 20,766 'retractables' the first year of prodcution, but interest faded and the retractable hardtop was discontinued after only a few years.

Above all, the 1950s offered more. More colors, more options and more variety. Long gone were the days when the only choice was the Model T. Now consumers could chose from convertibles, sedans, station wagons or sports cars.

THE THUNDERBIRD

In one race against Chevrolet, Ford was clearly the winner. In 1953, Chevrolet introduced a sports car, the Corvette, with the expectation that 10,000 cars would be sold. Ford responded two years later with the racy Thunderbird, which sold far better than Ford had dreamed—53,166 cars were sold in three years.

The Thunderbird had a choice of manual (plus overdrive) or automatic transmission. Like the Corvette, the Thunderbird had a 102-inch wheelbase, but it was over 12 inches longer. Though it was priced $200 more than

the Corvette, the Thunderbird offered more for the money. With its 292-ci (4.8-liter) Y-block V8 engine, the Thunderbird was capable of producing 202 hp—which pleased the sports car enthusiast who had been disappointed with the Corvette's performance.

A few minor changes were made over the next two years. In response to complaints about lack of storage space, the 1956 cars featured a 'continental kit' for spare tire storage. Also in 1956, the detachable hardtop was given a 'porthole' look. The following year the tailfins were emphasized and, even better, a 312-ci (5.1-liter) V8 engine was added as an option.

In 1958, the Thunderbird underwent a transformation from a two-seater sportscar to a fourseat 'personal car,' commonly known as a 'Squarebird.' The basic style would remain unchanged for the next three years. The new Thunderbird was obviously larger than its predecessor. The wheelbase increased from 102 to 113 inches, and the overall length from 181.4 to 205.4 inches. Weight jumped to 3900. The changes proved to be popular—sales of the 1958 model were twice that of the 1957 model, and in 1959 they were even better. With four sporty bucket seats, the Thunderbird was one-of-a-kind.

The restyled Thunderbird was powered by a 352-ci (5.8-liter), 300-hp V8, with a 430 (7.0-liter) capable of 350 hp as an option. Ford wasn't shy about proclaiming the virtues of the optional engine: 'Thunderbird's new optional 350-hp engine gives you the ultimate in action—a luxury car that is the peer of even sports cars in performance!' Most of the car-

buying public were not swayed by Ford's exciting claim. Car buffs, however, did take note. *Hot Rod* magazine tested the 1958 Thunderbird and it did 0-60 in nine seconds. The magazine commented that the 430 Thunderbird in standard form was not a screamer, but a change of axle ratios would improve the times and, with proper tuning, 'There is no reason why the Bird shouldn't be capable of holding its own with the other similarly equipped stockers running at the weekend drag races.'

In 1961, the Thunderbird entered another three-year styling period. The redesigned Thunderbird had smoother lines and a grille and bumper similar to that of the Lincoln Continental, which was produced at the same

Opposite, top: *The Lincoln has always maintained its image as a status symbol.*

Opposite, bottom: *A 1951 Ford Custom Fordor.*

Below: *Perfect for the suburbanite—the 1952 Ford Customline.*

At bottom: *With the start of the baby boom, many young families of the 1950s discovered that a station wagon, such as Ford's Country Squire, was a necessity.*

Ford introduced its first sports car—the Thunderbird—in 1955, and it immediately overtook the competition, Chevrolet's underpowered Corvette.

The 1957 model (below) is considered by collectors to be the most desirable year. With the optional 312-ci (5.1-liter) V8 engine, the T-Bird was even faster and more powerful than before. Above all, this was the last year the T-Bird was offered as a racy two-seater.

Above: *As Ford Motor Company's mid-priced mark, Mercury was doing well. By 1950, the one-millionth Mercury had been manufactured and a new factory was needed to keep up with demand. This is a 1953 Mercury sports coupe.*

Opposite, top: *A 1954 Ford Mainliner.*

Opposite, bottom: *A sporty Mercury Monterey convertible was the perfect car for a sunny summer day in the mid-1950s.*

plant. The weight went up about 150 pounds, while the power to haul it went down. Standard transmissions were replaced with Cruise-O-Matic, a three-speed automatic introduced with the 1958 models.

In 1962, the basic Thunderbird was unchanged, but two new models were introduced: the Landau hardtop and the Sports Roadster. In an attempt to recapture the magic of the two-seater 1955-57 T-Birds, the Sports Roadster had a removable fiberglass tonneau cover for the rear seats. To add to the sporty look, the Roadster also included Kelsey-Hayes wire wheels in chrome with knock-off-type hubcaps. Rear fender skirts were omitted to show off the wheels. Only 1427 Roadsters were produced in 1962 and even fewer in 1963, its last year of production.

In 1964, a new body shell was introduced. Slightly larger overall than the 1961-63 models, the 1964 T-Bird had more squared-off lines. The Sports Roadster model was discontinued, but pieces were available as options. Only about 45 convertibles left the factory with the Sports Roadster option, making them very rare indeed.

The 1964 model year signaled the end of the T-bird's era as a performance car. In the years to come the Thunderbird would undergo massive changes, eventually becoming a different breed of car altogether, but in those first few years of production a legend had been born.

THE FAIRLANE

Another car that helped Ford in the race to beat Chevrolet was the Fairlane. Introduced in November 1954, the Fairlane was glamourous, offering, according to Crusoe, 'all the desirable features we know how to put into a car.' Slightly larger than the 1954 Fords, the Fairlane had a new, low silhouette, a flatter hood, wraparound windshields and a longer rear deck. Available in a range of colors, it offered optional trim combinations and multiple choices in power services and air conditioning.

The Mainline, Ford's basic offering, however, failed to enjoy similar success. Several top officials at Ford believed that the public was no longer interested in low-priced cars. As the standard of living improved, people wanted more—better clothes, better homes and better cars.

THE EDSEL

The public's desire for a bigger, better car dovetailed with Ford's goal to increase its market share. The profits on an inexpensive car are clearly not as significant as those on a luxury sedan. At General Motors, the luxury divisions of Pontiac, Buick and Cadillac buoyed the profits of Chevrolet. At Ford, however, the Lincoln-Mercury Division failed to sell as well their counterparts at GM.

JR Davis decided the answer was to develop a medium-priced car that would be produced and sold within the Lincoln-Mercury Division. He proposed a car that was slightly larger than a Ford to compete with Pontiac and a second version that would be smaller than a Lincoln to compete with Buick.

Lewis Crusoe, head of the new Ford Division, had a far different idea. He envisioned a new division to handle the new car. Crusoe's position and success rate (the Thunderbird was his brainchild) carried clout with Henry Ford and Ernie Breech. He was in the number three position and in some ways was more in touch with the company's day-to-day operations than the two top men. Crusoe set up a task force to study the matter, placing Francis C 'Jack' Reith in charge.

Jack Reith, one of the original Whiz Kids, was riding high, having just resurrected Ford of France, long a sore point among the overseas subsidiaries. Reith presented his bold plan to the board of directors on 15 April 1955. He based his argument that Ford should enter the medium-priced market on these salient facts. Although Ford held 43.1 percent of sales in the low-priced popular market, with its Mercury and Lincoln cars it had only 13.6 percent. Moreover, there was a $700 gap between the top Mercury, at $2400, and the lowest price Lincoln, at $3100. Reith argued that when basic Ford buyers were ready to trade up, they turned to GM, which had three cars in the price range, or to Chrysler, which offered two cars. Ford Motor therefore needed to target this segment of the market with a car that was not a Ford, not a Mercury, not a Lincoln, but

something that was completely new and different.

The board of directors voted unanimously in favor of Reith's proposal, but he had laid his groundwork carefully, talking to each member prior to the meeting, winning their support in advance.

The Special Products Division under the direction of RE Krafve was set up to produce the new car. The E—for Experimental—car was underway, but thousands of details were yet to be decided, not the least of which was a name for the new car. The name had to excite the public without being overly exotic. It had to establish the new car as separate and distinct

In 1956, Dwight D Eisenhower was president, Elvis Presley was rockin' and rollin' and the Fairlane Victoria (opposite, top) *and the Fairlane Sunliner* (opposite, bottom) *were two of Ford's popular models.*

Ford Motor Company envisioned its customers moving up from the low-priced Ford Customline (below) *to the medium-priced Mercury Montclair* (above).

Pleas for the return of Edsel Ford's elegant Lincoln Continental of the early 1940s prompted Ford to bring out the Continental Mark II in 1956 (opposite top) and 1957 (opposite bottom).

Below: Front and rear views of the 1958 Thunderbird. Though car buffs of today fondly recall the two-seater Thunderbird of the mid-1950s, Ford's decision to turn the T-Bird into a larger 'personal car' was in tune with the times. Sales of the 1958 Thunderbird were almost double those of the previous year.

from the Ford, Lincoln and Mercury cars, while at the same time stating its identity as part of this reliable family.

The task of meeting all these conditions was given to David Wallace, who had been the force behind the selection of the Thunderbird name. For that task, Wallace had analyzed public response to the name, but for the E car, Wallace was looking for a muse and turned to poet Marianne Moore. Among the names she suggested were Resilient Bullet, Mongoose Civique, Andante con Moto, Varsity Stroke and Utopian Turtletop.

Meanwhile, Foote, Cone and Belding, a Chicago-based advertising agency, was compiling a list of 18,000 names, a selection of which were evaluated daily in a darkened room. Wallace would flash a name printed in six-inch tall block letters on a screen and wait for the audience to respond. When a name appealed to

someone in the audience, a voice from the crowd would yell 'Stop,' the lights would come on and a discussion of the name's merits would ensue. On one occasion, he flashed the word 'BUICK.' No response. By this time his audience was so tired of the process that many of them preferred to nap the time away.

After an entire year of research and analysis, Foote, Cone and Belding culled the list down to 6000, then 400, until finally all but four had been eliminated: Citation, Corsair, Ranger and Pacer. These four names later became the names for the model designations.

The final selections were presented to the executive committee. Henry and his brothers, Bill and Benson, were out of town, and Ernest Breech was chairing the meeting in Henry's absence. The executive committee was unimpressed with the choice of names, and Breech turned to the list of rejected names, picked one and said, 'Why don't we just call it Edsel?'

The three Ford brothers had been opposed to using their father's name, but when presented with the committee's decision, Henry reluctantly agreed to convince his brothers. David Wallace sent out market researchers to find out the 'immediate associations' the word Edsel produced. People on the street responded with such comments as 'schmedsel,' 'pretzel' and 'weasel.' A full 40 percent simply said 'What?'

In the meantime, the design of the E car was in the hands of Roy A Brown, Jr. Brown photographed the front grille of every car produced in Detroit. When the minor variations were overlooked, all the grilles had one thing in

Convertibles were extremely popular in the 1950s and though most were 'rag tops' like this (opposite top) 1957 Ford Fairlane 500, some models featured the unusual (above) retractable hardtop.

Below and opposite bottom: *The Lincoln Division produced Ford Motor Company's most expensive and exclusive cars, such as the Lincoln Premiere.*

equipped with a 345-hp engine, the most powerful available.

The Edsel was unveiled in late August 1957. As part of the publicity plans surrounding the Edsel's release, 75 cars were lent to auto writers who would drive the cars from Dearborn to their local Edsel dealerships, attracting attention along the way. The general public met the Edsel through a television extravaganza starring Bing Crosby.

Ford Motor Company projected first year sales at 200,000. Two years later roughly half that number had been sold. Part of the problem behind the poor sales was that the economic condition of the United States in 1957 was not what it had been in 1955, when Jack Reith had offered his proposal. Then, the medium-priced cars represented 40 percent of the market. In the meantime, the economy had experienced a downturn and the market share for a medium-priced car fell to 25 percent.

Contributing also to the Edsel's failure were numerous production problems. Most of the cars were produced on Ford and Mercury assembly lines rather than at an assembly plant dedicated to just Edsels. Every hour a single Edsel moved down the assembly line, frustrating the workers as they reached for the unaccustomed part and forcing them to increase their pace to handle the extra unit. Ford and Mercury did not change their production schedule to accommodate the Edsel. The workers were still expected to produce 60 Fords or Mercurys as well as the extra Edsel within an hour. As is often the case with a speed-up, the Edsel suffered.

The defective Edsels were bought back by Ford and subjected to expensive repairs. In an effort to make the car more appealing to the public, the horse collar grille was redesigned as quickly as possible, but nothing was able to boost sales and the Edsel, along with its division and dealerships, was discontinued after two years.

Another division to be discontinued about this time was the Continental Division, which was merged into the Lincoln Division. William Clay Ford, Edsel's youngest son, had carried on his father's work, styling the graceful Continental. On 6 October 1955, Billy Ford unveiled his Continental — the Continental Mark II. Inspired by the Lincoln Continental of 1940-1948, the new car was touted as the 'Rebirth of A Proud Tradition.' Exquisitely finished, quiet and lavishly equipped with items usually offered as options, the Mark II was vitually hand-built according to exacting specifications. It was also incredibly expensive and failed to reach the break even point.

The car had originally been seen as a loss leader that was intended to enhance the image of Ford Motor Company. But the original idea was revised as Ford made plans to offer its

common: the design was essentially horizontal. He proposed to create a new look — a single, vertical, bladelike structure. It was an innovative and dramatic design, but the engineers pointed out that it would cause ventilation problems for the engine, so the swordlike grille was hollowed out and transformed into an egg shape. When the car was on the market, the infamous grille would be compared to a toilet seat or a man sucking a lemon. Then the accountants started questioning the cost of each curve and scallop, and Brown's design underwent a number of subtle changes.

The final product had a horse-collar grille, double headlights, a gull-winged rear deck and scallops below. It featured several innovations, such as push buttons on the steering wheel for shifting gears instead of the conventional gear-shift lever, safety-rim wheels and self-adjusting brakes. Two models were

Today a collector's item, the Edsel was one of the all-time marketing fiascos. Ford created the Edsel Division to capture the medium-priced market, but the market had died by the time the Edsel was released. The new division built four models: the Ranger, the Pacer, the Corsair and the Citation. The two cars on the opposite page are 1958 Pacers. The car below is a 1959 Corsair. In an effort to please consumers, the 'horse-collar' grille was toned down for 1960 (above), but the Edsel had already sung its swan song.

stock to the public. As a public company, Ford would have to explain the losses of the Continental to its stockholders. Ernest Breech decided a better tactic would be to hide the losses in the more profitable Lincoln Division. Henry II agreed with Breech and on 18 July 1956 the Continental Division was absorbed into the Lincoln Division, effectively putting an end to Billy Ford's domain.

FORD GOES PUBLIC

With the creation of the Edsel Division, Ford Motor Company had attempted to become more like GM in structure, the hope being that they could beat the giant corporation at its own game. Clearly, other tactics were needed, not the least of which was to go public. Ford could not compete against GM unless it had the capital that only the open market could provide.

Years ago Edsel Ford and Ernest Kanzler had suggested that Ford become a publicly owned corporation. Family-owned companies were a thing of the past, but Old Henry had objected to the idea until his dying day. When Henry II assumed control, the way was clear for him to take the company public, a plan which was finally implemented in 1955.

The Ford Foundation was the key that enabled Ford Motor Company to offer its stock to the public while allowing the Ford family to maintain control of the company. The Ford Foundation had been formed in 1936. Because of high inheritance taxes, wealthy families often created foundations as a way to keep the money in the family. Thus, the purpose of a foundation was twofold—it contributed money to philanthropic causes while avoiding exorbitant government taxes. As a matter of principle, Henry I was as opposed to charitable organizations as he was to complex legal maneuverings, but when President Roosevelt increased income and inheritance taxes, Old Henry reconsidered his position, and the Ford Foundation came into being.

First, all the company's existing stocks were converted to two classes: A and B. Class A stock consisted of 95 percent of the old stock but carried no voting power. The Class B—the remaining five percent of the stock—carried all the voting power. In other words, the family could lose 95 percent of its stock and still control the company.

Below: Two-tone paint jobs were fashionable throughout the 1950s.

As the 1950s drew to a close, the Mercury Division offered such cars as the 1958 Park Lane sedan (opposite top) *and the 1959 Colony Park station wagon* (opposite bottom), *with its trendy wood trim.*

Next, the Ford Foundation was established 'to receive and administer funds for scientific, educational and charitable purposes, all for the public welfare and for no other purpose.' Donations to charities are exempt from taxes, so the Fords could will their Class A stock to the newly created foundation, thereby avoiding a tax on 95 percent of their wealth *while* maintaining voting control.

With the deaths of Edsel, Henry and Clara (who died in 1950), the Ford Foundation became a major philanthropic organization in the early 1950s. Although endowed with a vast fortune, the foundation had no control over its wealth. It was subject to the whims of the auto industry. If Ford Motor Company prospered, so did the foundation. If Ford foundered, so too would the foundation. The solution was to diversify its assets by selling Ford stock and reinvesting the proceeds, but the stocks were not traded on the open market.

The problem in going public was how to maintain family control of Ford. Through a series of complicated stock reclassifications, the family retained two-fifths of the voting power, while three-fifths was to be divided among the general public. Though this voting structure may not seem like an equitable arrangement, the public did not hesitate to acquire stock in Ford Motor Company.

From that November day in 1955 when the Ford Foundation announced that seven million shares of Ford Motor Company stock would be available, the public's enthusiasm was unbounded. Switchboards at brokerages were jammed, and 722 underwriters were enlisted to

handle incoming orders. Trading began on 17 January 1956 at $64.50 a share. By the end of the day, the price had risen to $70.50, and the Ford Foundation had $640,000,000 in its coffers.

People who previously had no interest in the stock market wanted a piece of Ford Motor Company. Ford stock represented the legacy of Henry Ford, the last of the American heroes. Many people were buying the stock, not for themselves, but for their children and their grandchildren, for their nieces and their nephews. The stock was a piece of the American dream, and men and women across the country were buying it for the future of America.

A NEW ERA

When Ford went public in 1956, Ernest Breech went from executive vice president to chairman of the board of directors, which meant that Breech, not Henry Ford II, addressed the annual meeting of shareholders. Henry clearly chafed at playing second fiddle, if only temporarily. But the situation was symptomatic of a deeper change in the relationship between Henry and Ernie. The two disagreed on various matters of policy, something unheard of in the past. Ernest Breech had come to Ford Motor Company to help Henry Ford rebuild the company. Breech had been an able mentor, and it was clear that his student had learned his lessons well. In July 1960, Ernest Breech submitted his resignation as chairman of the Ford Motor Company.

For a few months Henry acted as both chairman and president. Then, on 9 November 1960, *Chairman* Henry Ford II announced that he would be assisted by *President* Robert S McNamara. A member of the Whiz Kids, McNamara was known for his intelligence and for his determination in getting a job done. 'Put in value, not cost' was McNamara's creed. As head of the Ford Division, McNamara had overseen the refinement of the 1957 Fairlane. The 1957 offering featured whitewalls, tinted glass, an electric clock, a radio and a two-tone finish. The most lavishly equipped car that Ford had ever offered, the 1957 Fairlane was priced at only $2556. That year the Ford Division reached its long-sought goal of beating Chevrolet, selling 1,493,627 Fords to 1,456,288 Chevrolets.

THE FALCON

McNamara had also masterminded the development of the 1960 Ford Falcon, a practical, compact car that provided basic family transportation. It was the sort of car that Henry I would have heartily approved, and like Henry's Model T, the Falcon was incredibly successful, selling a record 417,000 cars in its

Facing page: Reliable and economical, the Ford Falcon was the perfect family car. Introduced in 1960, the Falcon's popularity rivaled that of the Model T and became the standard by which Ford would measure the success of each subsequent release.

The Falcon was developed by Robert McNamara, who had joined the company shortly after Henry II took over. McNamara rose through the ranks, eventually becoming president of Ford.

first year. The Falcon was priced to compete with the small imports, which had already gained a 10 percent share of the market. But the Falcon had a decided advantage over the imports—it could hold six passengers, making it large enough for many American families.

The Falcon was simple in style as well as engineering. The engine was a front-mounted lightweight, 144-ci (2.4-liter) short-stroke six that put out 90 hp. The front suspension was coils and shocks mounted over the upper A-frame, with leaf springs in the rear. The consumer could chose a three-speed manual or a two-speed Ford-o-Matic transmission. The Falcon sat on a 109.5-inch wheelbase.

The Falcon offered excellent mileage and had an excellent reputation as a trouble free car. If repairs were necessary, the car's simple design kept the cost low. Insurance companies even offered a discount to people who drove a Falcon.

Recognizing that it had a hit on its hands with the Falcon, Ford introduced another compact car, the Comet, later in 1960. The Comet used the same components as the Falcon and was, essentially, a stretched Falcon. Orininally a product of the Ford Divison, the Comet started wearing the Mercury nameplate in 1962. Cheaper to run and easier to park than the average American automobile, these two small cars were harbingers of things to come, but, as time would tell, the Big Three would belatedly heed the call for compact cars. The Comet, in fact, would be redesigned as a mid-size car in 1966. Then, in 1971, it would again appear as a compact.

At top: *One of the 'Big Ms,' the 1960 Mercury Monterey 2-door hardtop rested on a 126-inch wheelbase. At the other end of the spectrum, the Ford Falcon (above) rode on a 110-inch span.*

Previous pages: *With its new sleek lines, the 1962 Thunderbird was a hit with sports car enthusiasts.*

As successful as the Falcon was, it wasn't a money-maker for Ford. An economical car without many income-generating options, the Falcon just didn't bring in revenue.

The Falcon's success earned Robert McNamara the presidency of Ford, but McNamara was president of Ford Motor Company for less than two months. John F Kennedy had just been elected President of the United States, and he wanted McNamara as part of his cabinet. McNamara accepted, serving as Secretary of Defense until 1968.

With McNamara's resignation, John Dykstra, formerly the production manager, was appointed president of Ford. Dykstra, a one-time GM man, had been with Ford since 1947, and as president he continued to focus on getting the product to market on time and within the budget. The end result was that Henry as chairman had greater involvement in the management of Ford—which was exactly what he wanted.

An equally significant appointment was the man chosen to head the Ford Division, the spot vacated by McNamara initially. In fact, McNamara himself had recommended the man to take his place—Lee Iacocca.

Lido Anthony Iacocca, the son of an Italian immigrant, was an engineering student at Lehigh University when a recruiter drove through the campus in a Mark I Lincoln Continental. 'That car really turned my head,' Iacocca recalled in his autobiography. 'One glimpse of it and one whiff of the leather interior were enough to make me want to work at Ford for the rest of my life.'

Iacocca started working for Ford Motor Company in December 1946, after he finished his master's degree at Princeton. He started in a training program for engineers, but it didn't take him long to decide that the quickest way to climb to the top was in sales. For the next 10 years he was out in the field, hustling. He developed a knack for selling and was promoted to teaching how to sell.

Iacocca attracted the attention of top Ford officials in 1956. Ford had decided to promote auto safety, rather than performance and hp. The campaign was a disaster, and all across the United States, Fords were selling poorly—except in Pennsylvania, where Iacocca, the district sales manager had devised a gimmicky plan for selling cars. With a 20 percent down payment, the consumer could drive away a new Ford and have 36 monthly payments of only $56. Iocacca's rallying cry of '56 for 56' was selling Fords in Philadelphia while the rest of the country was in a slump.

As an additional come-on he added a bag of potato chips bearing the words 'The chips are down. We're selling cars for $56 a month.' He also devised the 'wujatak' card, pronounced 'would ya take.' The plan was for Ford salesmen to drive around supermarket parking lots, armed with wujutaks, looking for well-cared for cars. When they spotted a likely car, they looked up the car's value in the secondhand-car price guide and on the back of the wujatak

Below: *For 1960, the Ford Galaxie swelled to a 119-inch wheelbase and some models got a sleek semi-fastback Starliner hardtop. Though not as popular as the square-roof styles, the shape of the Starliner was just the thing for NASCAR racing.*

Ford unveiled its Galaxie 500 XL series in the spring of 1962. The '500' symbolized the 500-mile NASCAR races Ford was winning, while the 'XL' stood for 'Xtra Lively.' The XL's standard powerplant was a 292 (4.8-liter) V8 with 170-bhp, but the optional 352s (5.8-liter) and 390s (6.4-liter) could turn the Galaxie into a real fire-breather, especially when teamed with a Borg-Warner four-speed gearbox. The sportiest of the full-sized Fords, the 500 XL offered luxury and power to boot.

Left: *A close-up of the dash of a 1963 Galaxie 500 XL.*

Right: *A 1963 Galaxie 500 XL 2-door hardtop.*

Below: *The 500 XL for 1966, with a big 428 (7.0-liter) V8.*

card wrote up an offer for the car in exchange for a new Ford. When the shoppers returned to their cars, they found the wujatak offer and a bag of chips.

Crazy as it sounds, the '56 for 56' campaign worked. In short order, the Philadelphia district was the top-selling area, and Robert McNamara, then head of the Ford Division, decided to implement Iacocca's sales plan, minus the potato chips, nationwide. Thanks to Iacocca's wacky scheme, sales improved, albeit late in the year. McNamara credited the plan with selling as many as 75,000 cars.

Lee Iacocca's reward was a transfer to Ford headquarters in Dearborn to manage Ford truck marketing. Four years later Henry Ford summoned Iacocca to his office and made

him the general manager of the Ford Division, with its attendant title of vice president. He was only 36 years old and seen by many as too young to handle such a major responsibility, but Robert McNamara wanted the man who had dreamed up '56 for 56' on his team. Though McNamara himself was on the team only a few months before he left for Washington, his decision to promote Iacocca would have a profound effect on the history of Ford Motor Company.

Over the next few years, Iacocca proved to be a whiz at taking the basic product and adding a few extras that added appeal as well as profits. He turned the dependable Falcon into a convertible and offered it with a V8 engine option to appeal to the muscle car

crowd. For the Thunderbird, he developed a limited Monaco Edition with a white leather interior and special numbered brass plate.

In April 1963, Lee Iacocca launched Ford's Total Performance Project with a speech about factory involvement in motor racing. Iacocca said that Ford believed that racing improves the breed and that anybody entering a racing event using a Ford car or Ford power deserved factory support. In short, he was explaining that Ford intended to use race successes as part of its advertising campaign, and thus was born the 'race on Sunday, sell on Monday' slogan.

In essence, Ford was capitalizing on a strength that had gone unheeded for the last few years. Hot rodders had long ago discov-

ered Ford's flathead V8. In 1960, Ford had introduced the 352 High-Performance engine that would be the basis of the Super/Stock class. Other makers had put out high performance engines with high-compression pistons, hot cams, dual carburetors and dual exhausts, but Ford had refined and strengthened the engine so that it would not come apart at the seams. This engine was the basis of the later hot engines, such as the 406 and the 427. Ford made a strong appearance on the NASCAR ovals with these engines, often under the hood of a Fairlane—in a break from its usual role as the family sedan. Falcons and Galaxies joined the Fairlanes on the drag strip, establishing themselves as legends of the 'Muscle Car' era.

Impressive as these cars were, there was one car that could beat them all—the Ford AC Cobra.

The Cobra was the work of Carroll Shelby, a successful race car driver who had to quit racing when he developed a heart condition. Originally from Texas, Shelby had visitied racetracks around the world and was well aware of the ability of European cars to outmaneuver American cars. On the other hand, America's big V8s were unbeatable. Shelby was determined to create a car with both characteristics.

Body and chassis were supplied by the AC company of Thames Ditton, England, while the engines came from the Ford Motor Company. The first power plant he installed in the AC carbody was a 260-ci (4.3-liter) V8, which went into only 75 Cobras, before being replaced by a 289. Ultimately, the Cobra was powered by Ford's 427—and there was no stopping it. Shelby had vowed 'to blow Ferrari's ass off' and the 427 did just that. Shelby withdrew the Cobra from competition in 1965, but that was not the end of his relationship with Ford. Lee Iacocca's latest and greatest creation—the Mustang—would also profit from the skilled hand of Carroll Shelby.

Above: *With a 390-ci (6.4-liter) V8 under the hood, the 1966 Ford Fairlane GT/A coupe lived a dual life as family car and muscle car.*

Far left: *By 1967, the Thunderbird had grown considerably longer and larger, and was now firmly entrenched in the personal-luxury market it helped to create.*

THE MUSTANG

Numerous legends surround the development of the Mustang. One story claims that the Mustang was the result of intensive market research by Iacocca. Such factors as baby boomers coming of age, college graduates with more disposable income, and families looking for second cars that were both fun and easy to maneuver all pointed to the need for a small, sporty car.

According to the other version of the legend, the Mustang was born in Ford's design studio in response to Chevrolet's Monza, a sporty version of the Corvair. Ford's answer was the handiwork of Gene Bordinant and Don DeLaRossa. They took Ford's 289-ci (4.7-liter) V8 engine and devised a new shell to give it a look of power—a two-seater with a long hood, a squared roof and a low, flat rear deck.

Whether the Mustang, then known as the Allegro, was the result of market research or a reply to Chevrolet hardly matters. The Mustang became Lee Iacocca's success story. When he saw the clay version decked out in red, he knew he could sell it. But first he had to sell it to Henry Ford, and Henry was still smarting from the failure of the Edsel.

The first time Iacocca presented Henry with the idea for a new car, Henry walked away, refusing to listen. The second time, in the spring of 1962, Iacocca got his attention with a visual demonstration of Ford's need for a new car. He lined up all the Ford models and across from each car was the equivalent Chevrolet competitor. But Chevy's Monza stood alone. When Henry Ford *saw* that Ford had no entry in the growing youth market, he agreed to Iacocca's proposal. After climbing into the car, he announced 'It's a little tight in the back seat. Add another inch for leg room.'

Lee Iacocca had Henry's approval. Now he needed a name for his new car, which is often the hardest part to get right because it is such an emotional decision. At first, the car was called the Special Falcon and then the Cougar. Henry Ford suggested the T-Bird II. Finally, the

Facing page: *In 1965, America's on-going love affair with the automobile entered a new phase when Ford unveiled the Mustang.*

By tapping into an undiscovered market segment, sales of the Mustang were no less than phenomenal. The greatest single automotive success story of the 1960s, the Mustang sold 418,812 units it first year of production, setting an all-time record for first-year sales of a new model.

choices were narrowed down to Monte Carlo, Monaco, Torino and Cougar. The first two names were already registered with the Automobile Manufacturers Association, so that left Torino and Cougar. Torino, the Italian spelling for the town of Turin, was selected because it evoked the foreign flavor that Ford hoped it had captured with the new car. As a compromise to those who had favored Cougar as a name, a stylized cougar would be the Torino's emblem.

Iacocca soon received word from the public relations department that he would have to choose a new name. Henry Ford was in the midst of a divorce and seeing an Italian woman, Cristina Vettore Austin. Public relations feared that a car with an Italian name might lead to unfavorable publicity.

Finding a new name took on a sense of urgency, and Iacocca turned to John Conley of Ford's ad agency, J Walter Thompson, for help. Conley, who had previously researched bird names for the Falcon and the Thunderbird, came back with a list of thousands of animal names. Once again, the list of final selections was pared down to just a few names: Bronco, Puma, Cheetah, Colt, Mustang and, again, Cougar. The new car was christened Mustang.

Mustang had been the designation for one of the car's prototypes, and the name referred to the legendary World War II fighter plane—not the horse. Nonetheless, a galloping horse was chosen as the car's emblem.

In 20 months, the Mustang was ready. The team that Iacocca had assembled to produce the car was hard-working. They worked late

The early Mustangs were available in three body styles: hardtop (far right), convertible or fastback coupe (see page 130-131).

Convertibles, like the 1966 model above, were rare and are highly prized collector's items today.

and met every Saturday morning at the Fairlane Hotel, and thanks to their dedication and thoroughness, the Mustang—unlike the Edsel—was introduced to the public with all the bugs ironed out.

The Mustang was unveiled at the New York World's Fair in April 1964. Cars are normally introduced in the fall of the year, but Iacocca and his team believed that their car was so new and exciting that they changed the rules to fit the car. While these cars were technically known as 1965 models, Mustang enthusiasts refer to them as 1964 1/2 releases because they differ in some respects from the Mustangs that were built after August 1965.

Lee and his team decided that only the World's Fair had the drama and excitement to unveil the car of their dreams—which instantly became the car of everyone's dreams. The Mustang cost less than $2500, and even though it was an inexpensive car, Ford wanted it to appeal to customers who wanted luxury, so every model had bucket seats, vinyl trim, wheel covers and carpeting as standard features.

In addition, over 50 options were available and consumers tended to add the options of their choice, boosting the profits of an already

successful car. Over 80 percent added white sidewall tires, 80 percent wanted radios and 71 percent ordered eight-cylinder engines. Every tenth customer drove out with a 'Rallye Pack'—a tachometer and a clock. On the average, customers added $1000 to the base price of $2368.

Ford launched a massive campaign to promote the Mustang. The company invited various editors of college newspapers to Dearborn and gave them a Mustang to drive for a few weeks. Four days before the car was introduced, one hundred members of the press took part in a huge Mustang rally from New York to Dearborn. In testimony of the Mustang's reliability, all 70 cars handled the journey without a single problem.

On the day of its release—17 April 1964—there was at least one Mustang at every one of the 8160 Ford dealerships across the country. All over the United States, people rushed to their local Ford dealer. In Chicago, one dealer had to lock his showroom because he couldn't handle the crowds. In Pittsburgh, another dealership was so overflowing with customers that there wasn't enough room to remove the lone Mustang from the wash rack. A Ford dealer in Garland, Texas sold his single Mus-

These pages: In 1968, the Mustang made a serious play for muscle car dominance with optional big-block engines: a 335hp 390-ci (6.4 liter) and a 390hp 427-ci (7.0-liter).

tang to the highest bidder, and the customer insisted on spending the night in the car so that no one else could lay claim to it while his check was clearing the bank. And in Seattle, the driver of a passing cement truck was so mesmerized by the sporty Mustang on display that he crashed through the showroom window. During the Mustang's first weekend on sale, *four million* people visited Ford dealerships.

As part of its advertising campaign, Ford ran full-page ads in 2600 newspapers on the day the car was released. Television was bombarded with Mustang commercials, and Mustangs were on display at 15 of the country's busiest airports and in the lobbies of 200 Holiday Inns.

Some of the best advertising came from *Time* and *Newsweek*, which ran simultaneous cover stories on the Mustang. *Time* declared

that 'Iacocca had produced more than just another new car. With its long hood and short rear deck, its Ferrari flair and openmouthed air scoop, the Mustang resembles the European racing cars that American sports car buffs find so appealing. Yet Iacocca had made the Mustang's design so flexible, its price so reasonable, and its options so numerous that its potential appeal reaches toward two-thirds of all US car buyers. Priced as low as $2368 and able to accommodate a small family in its four seats, the Mustang seems destined to be a sort of Model A of sports cars—for the masses as well as the buffs.'

After the car had been on the market for only a few weeks, Ford realized it would far exceed its initial sales projection of 75,000 units and converted a second plant in San Jose, California to Mustang production. Later, a third plant in Metuchen, New Jersey was converted.

Above: *The Mustang underwent its first facelift in 1969 with the Mach I. Longer, lower and wider, the body featured dummy hood scoops and vents and a rear spoiler. This is a 1972 Mach I fastback.*

Opposite top: *A 1972 Mustang Sportsroof coupe.*

Right: *As the Mustang of the early 1970s got bigger, its popularity declined. The era of the pony car was over.*

Whether the legendary market research came before or after the fact, the Mustang did indeed fill the niche for the small-sporty segment of the market. Iocacca's dream was for the Mustang to break all Ford's sales records the first year of its release. To do that, the Mustang would have to best the Falcon's first year sales of 417,154 cars. On 16 April 1965, the 418,812th was sold. In both 1965 and 1966, the Mustang sold over half a million cars. Sales of the Mustang in 1966—its best year, with 549,400 units sold—represented 6.1 percent of all cars sold in North America and an incredible 78.2 percent of the small-sporty segment. In its first two years, the Mustang generated net profits of $1.1 billion.

Henry Ford was thrilled with the success of the new little car and justly rewarded the man responsible with a promotion to the position of Vice President, Cars and Trucks. Lee Iacocca, the salesman from Allentown, Pennsylvania, now supervised all Ford cars and trucks, as well as those of Lincoln-Mercury.

While Lee Iacocca climbed the ladder of success at Ford, his baby slowly but surely declined in popularity. By 1970, sales of the Mustang fell to 150,000—and understandably so. The little Mustang kept growing and growing, until it was eight inches longer and almost 600 pounds heavier.

Late in 1969, Iacocca mapped out a plan to revive slackened sales with the Mustang II. The car did well, but never equalled the success of its predecessor.

POWER STRUGGLE

When Henry Ford promoted Lee Iacocca to Vice-president, Cars and Trucks, he told Iacocca to 'rub some of that Mustang ointment onto the Lincoln-Mercury Division.' Lee did just that.

The Lincoln-Mercury Division had been part of Ford since the 1940s, but the division had never lived up to the company's expectations. Ford envisioned its satisfied customers eventually trading up to the higher-priced, luxury cars of the Lincoln-Mercury Division. Instead, they traded up to a GM car—a Buick, an Oldsmobile, or a Cadillac.

In 1965, Lee Iacocca set to work to revive the flagging sales of the ailing division. What Lincoln-Mercury needed more than anything else were new products, and by 1967, two new cars were ready: the Mercury Cougar and the Mercury Marquis.

THE MERCURY COUGAR

During its development stage, the Ford Mustang had briefly been known as the Cougar, and in the Mercury incarnation, the Cougar was intended to capture the Mustang driver who was ready for something a little plusher. Like the Mustang, the Cougar had a long hood and short deck.

After enduring a long period of the doldrums, the Mercury dealers were ready for an exciting new car, and the Mercury Cougar lived up to its dramatic unveiling.

In those days, Detroit introduced its new models at spectacular Las Vegas shows, complete with dancing girls, strobe lights, smoke bombs and various other special effects. The shows motivated the dealers and generated enthusiasm for the new cars among the general public. In September, Ford Motor Company took its top Mercury sales personnel on a cruise of the Caribbean, where it planned to unveil its new cars.

In an extravaganza befitting a Hollywood movie premiere, the Cougar was introduced to

Facing page: In 1968, Lee Iacocca decided to create the ultimate luxury car—a successor to Edsel's Lincoln Continental of 1940 and William Clay Ford's Lincoln Continental Mark II of 1956. Design chief Gene Bordinat followed the classic Continental tradition and gave the Mark a long hood/short deck, while assistant Hermann Brunn adorned the interior with large, comfortable bucket seats and a wood-grained dash.

The Mark III did far better than Ford had dreamed, outselling the competition—GM's popular Cadillac Eldorado.

the dealers on a torch-lit beach on the island of St Thomas in the Virgin Islands. A World War II landing craft pulled alongside the shore, lowered its ramp and a sparkling white Cougar drove off onto the beach. When the car came to a halt, entertainer Vic Damone stepped out and broke into song. The dealers knew they had a winner on their hands—and they were absolutely right.

To promote the new Mercury Cougar on television, Ford decided to use—what else?—a live cougar. Of course, training a cougar to walk across the Lincoln-Mercury sign posed a few problems, but once the sequence was finally filmed it proved so effective that 'the sign of the cat' came to represent not only the Cougar but the entire Lincoln-Mercury Division as well.

THE MARQUIS

The Marquis was introduced to the dealers under equally theatrical circumstances. While on the same Caribbean cruise that unveiled the Mercury, the dealers were all assembled on the stern of the ship. As the sun set, hundreds of helium balloons were released, revealing the 1967 Mercury Marquis.

The Marquis, a full-size luxury car, was intended to capture a share of the Buick and Oldsmobile market. Ford officials were convinced that the best way to sell the Marquis was to emphasize the car's smooth ride, so they proved their point to the advertising agency by blindfolding the account executives and taking them for a ride in Oldsmobiles, Buicks, Cadillacs and a Marquis. All but one

Below: *The Mercury Cougar was a luxury version of the Ford Mustang. Mechanically, the two cars were nearly identical, but the exterior of the Mercury was sleeker and smoother than its cousin's.*

Far right: *Introduced in 1968, the Torino was part of the muscle car craze. The GT line came equipped with a 302 V8, bucket seats, pinstriping and a long list of performance options.*

thought the Marquis gave the smoothest ride. Kenyon & Eckhardt worked the blindfold idea into their ad campaign in a series of commercials in which blindfolded consumers and, in one case, chauffeurs, judged cars on the basis of their smooth and quiet rides. In another series of commercials, the smooth ride of the Marquis was even more graphically demonstrated by performing a seemingly impossible act as the Marquis sped on its way. In one commercial, a record was playing on a phonograph on the front seat, while in another a barber was shaving football player Bart Starr. Another commercial featured a container of acid hanging above a fur coat. Yet another showed a diamond cutter at work as the Marquis maneuvered over a bumpy road. Perhaps the most dramatic finish belonged to the ad with the nitroglycerin on the back seat. To prove that the nitroglycerin was real, the car was blown up!

The Marquis and the Cougar helped to revive the Mercury line, but Lincoln still needed resuscitation. One night, while on the road, Lee Iacocca had a vision of a Rolls-Royce grille on a Thunderbird and immediately called designer Gene Bordinant to translate the

vision into reality. Taking his inspiration from the Continental Mark that Edsel Ford had designed in the 1930s and the Mark II designed by Edsel's son William Clay in the 1950s, Lee Iacocca decided it was time to bring out the Mark III. Envisioning a truly luxurious car—the Rolls-Royce of American autos—Iacocca began with the Thunderbird shell, making enough modifications that the car truly looked like a new and different car.

THE MARK III

Introduced in April 1968, the Mark III had a long hood, a short deck and the signature spare tire in the back. Powered by a V8, the new Mark created a striking image. Ford wanted the Mark to be seen as the epitome of good taste and planned to unveil the car at a midnight supper at Cartier's on Fifth Avenue in New York. Cartier's was interested in Ford's idea until it found out that the plan would necessitate a few walls being torn down. The store did, however, lend its name to the Mark III's clock.

Even though the plan for introducing the Mark III at Cartier's fell through, Ford came up

Above: *The Mercury Cougar followed a path similar to the Mustang, growing longer and larger. After its first facelift in 1971, the Cougar lost its sporty image and felt more like a family sedan, inside and out.*

with equally theatrical introductions in various cities across the United States. In Hollywood, for example, the car was placed on the set of *Camelot* and people had to climb a long flight of stairs to see it, just as they would if paying homage to a king. In Detroit, the traditional approach of placing the new car on a turntable was reversed, and the crowd, a group of newspaper publishers, was on the turntable. As the turntable slowly revolved, they saw a succession of vintage Lincolns and Marks. Finally, a curtain opened, revealing the new Lincoln Continental Mark III. Ford obviously achieved the desired effect, for several in the crowd ordered a new Mark on the spot.

The Mark III was wildly successful, doing far better than Ford had dared to hope. In its first year, the Mark outsold GM's Cadillac Eldorado. At a profit of $2000 per car, one Mark generated as much revenue as 10 Falcons. More significantly, the division was turning a profit for the first time since Ford had acquired the Lincoln company in the 1920s.

Iacocca had once again proven his skill at creating a winner, and he had done it for only $30 million—which was an incredibly low price for retooling and manufacturing a new model. Given his track record, Lee Iacocca was more than a little upset when Henry Ford announced that Semon E 'Bunkie' Knudsen would be the new president of Ford Motor Company. Bunkie Knudsen was the son of William Knudsen, who had once worked with Henry I, building assembly plants and Eagle boats. Henry I fired Knudsen, but Knudsen had his revenge when he joined General Motors and made Chevrolet the top automaker and himself president. Later, Bunkie had followed in his father's footsteps, rising through the ranks almost to the summit of the presidency. But Ed Cole became president of GM and three months later Bunkie was president of Ford.

Henry Ford was eager to capture some of the GM magic and he saw Bunkie as the key. However, he didn't want to lose Lee Iacocca, so he sent a company DC-3 to pick up Lee, who was on vacation with his family. Henry Ford essentially told Iacocca that his day would come. And it would.

According to Lee Iacocca, Bunkie had 'little impact on the company.' Bunkie, however, did not intend to sit around unnoticed, so he went straight to where things do get noticed—the styling studio. The design for the 1970 Thunderbird was completed, but that didn't stop Bunkie. He made the front end five inches shorter and changed its shape and modified the taillights. The end result was strangely reminiscent of a Pontiac. Then he turned his attention to the Mustang, adding more weight.

With the 1971 models, Bunkie had more time to leave his mark on the new cars, oftentimes re-doing what Iacocca had already approved, and so the frictions between Bunkie and Lee increased. Henry mediated a short-lived truce between his top executives, but the conflict continued when the 1972 cars were being designed.

This time, Iacocca went directly to Henry with his complaints and the chairman of the board was more sympathetic than Lee had hoped. Henry himself had been perturbed when Bunkie had given the final okay to the 1971 line. While technically that was Bunkie's job, it was a privilege that Henry had enjoyed since 1945.

In September 1969, 18 months after his arrival, Henry Ford fired Bunkie Knudsen. In his place, Henry set up a three-man office of the president. Lee Iacocca supervised Ford's North American operations; Robert Stevenson was in charge of Ford International; and Robert J Hampson headed Philco-Ford and tractor operations.

Fifteen months later, on 19 December 1970, Henry Ford walked into Lee Iacocca's office and granted Lee his long-cherished dream—the presidency of Ford. Today, the second in command, perhaps someday number one? Iacocca, as well as much of the auto industry, assumed that is how things would work out.

Below: *The Continental Mark tradition continued in 1971 with the Mark IV, still wearing its trademark sparetire kit in the back. This is a 1972 model.*

Below: With the passing of the muscle era, the Ford Torino traded its performance image for a plusher look and became the Gran Torino.

Far right: The energy crisis was just around the corner and Mercury would discover that cars like its 1972 Montego Brougham sedan were no longer what consumers wanted.

Much has been written about the conflict that ensued between Henry Ford and his heir apparent. Some accounts claim that Lee Iacocca started acting like he, not Henry, was running the company, that he was an egomaniac who abused the privileges of his position. Lee Iacocca's autobiography paints a different picture. According to Lee, Henry was paranoid, a bigot and a hypocrite who was out to destroy him.

Clearly, there was a great deal of animosity between the two men, but the truth undoubtedly lies somewhere between these two extreme points of view. Perhaps it simply boils down to the fact that, for all its size, Ford Motor Company was essentially a family company and Henry Ford was not ready to hand the reins of power over to someone outside of the family.

On 14 April 1977 Henry Ford held a press conference to announce that the management consulting firm of McKinsey and Company had recommended a reorganization of top management and, based on their findings, he was establishing a three-man Office of the Chief Executive. He would remain chairman, Iacocca would remain president, but a new position would be created: vice chairman. The new vice chairman was Philip Caldwell, who had enjoyed success as the head of Ford of Europe and since his return to Detroit had managed all of Ford Motor Company's international operations.

Henry Ford had used a triumvirate before, back when he had fired Bunkie Knudsen, and it seems probable that the McKinsey and Company recommendation was merely a political maneuver, an idea that gained credence a year later when Henry Ford fired Lee Iacocca. Caldwell was thus positioned to succeed Henry Ford upon his retirement, which was planned for 1980. However, in the summer of 1979 Henry Ford developed heart problems and decided to ensure Caldwell's succession. In October 1979, Henry appointed Philip Caldwell president and the following March named him chairman as well. Henry continued to serve on the board of directors, but for the first time on its 77-year history, the chief executive of Ford Motor Company was not a Ford.

OVERSEAS INVASION

Since the early 1950s, the number of foreign cars imported into the United States had been increasing steadily. At first the numbers were small. Aficionados of European luxury sedans and sport cars were an elitist group, but soon others were captivated by a different breed of import—the economy car.

In 1950, the Volkswagen Beetle sold a mere 300 cars in the United States. Detroit never figured that small imports would challenge its position. Big cars were part of the American identity, or so claimed a 1952 report by the Ford Division that stated 'To the average American, our present car and its size represent an outward symbol of prestige and well-being.'

The Big Three automakers ignored the signs. In 1953, the Volkswagen Beetle sold 2500 cars, still a small number, but by 1958, the figure had jumped to 104,000, and Volkswagen made up only a portion of the 379,000 imports sold in the United States. The following year, the figure skyrocketed to 614,000.

Detroit still failed to see the significance of the public's interest in imports. The auto industry refused to admit that foreign cars might be better made than American cars and that they were built to last longer. They didn't rust out or rattle like American cars, and they offered better gas mileage. But when Detroit examined the competition, it saw cars that were unsafe, unreliable, and difficult and expensive to repair—and it tried its best to convey that opinion to the American public.

Detroit begrudgingly responded with a few cars. In 1957 American Motors introduced America's first compact economy car, the Rambler, and a few years later General Motors brought out the Chevrolet Corvair. Ford Motor Company had its economical Falcon, which did sell phenomenally well. But Detroit was missing the big picture. Economy cars weren't just for a few eccentric Americans—they were the wave of the future.

By the mid-1960s, Detroit was enjoying a

Facing page: In the early 1970s, Detroit finally heeded the public's desire for an economy car. Ford Motor Company's entry into the subcompact race was the infamous Pinto. In theory, the Pinto was an excellent idea. In practice, however, the car's poor design was an unqualified disaster.

period of prosperity. In 1965, domestic car sales reached a record-breaking 8.8 million, while imports sales totaled only 570,000—a negligible increase over the previous five years. Detroit was feeling confident and perhaps just a little self-righteous. So instead of concentrating on the competition from abroad, Ford kept on producing its midsized Fairlanes and fullsized Galaxies and LTDs. By 1968, however, sales of imports exceeded the one million mark, and Detroit belatedly took notice.

THE MAVERICK

Ford responded with the Maverick in the spring of 1969. Gene Bordinant, head of the design department, was given the challenge of designing a car that was aesthetically pleasing to the consumer and economically feasible for Ford. He came up with a sporty, two-door model on a 103-inch wheelbase. Lee Iacocca liked the design, and so did Henry Ford, but Henry also wanted a four-door model. For the four-door model to have the same lines and look as the two-door version did it would have to be built on a 107-inch wheelbase, which essentially meant another car and a higher cost.

The only logical thing for Ford to do was build the two different models on the same wheelbase, allowing for interchangeable parts and a lower investment. Both Iacocca and Bordinant were opposed to the 107-inch wheelbase, arguing that the 103 would be sportier and less expensive to build. They finally con-

Above: *Falling sales of full-sized Galaxies and other gas guzzlers inspired Ford to develop the Maverick, a sporty little number that sat on a 103-inch wheelbase.*

Center and left: *Ford had high hopes for the Pinto. It seemed to be just what the public wanted. Small and easy to maneuver, the Pinto promised upwards of 25 miles per gallon in city driving. Tragically, the flaws in its innovative design were not discovered until it was too late and several people had been killed in car accidents involving Pintos.*

verted Henry Ford to their point of view. The Maverick would be a two-door on a 103-inch wheelbase, roughly eight inches longer than the Volkswagen Beetle and eight inches shorter than the standard Falcon.

Priced under $2000, the Maverick was, to quote Bordinant, 'sassy.' It had a short rear deck and a slanting European-style hood, but as its name was meant to convey that this car was all American. Hoping to repeat the success it had with the Mustang, Ford chose another name that evoked the American West. And just to hedge the bet a little, the Maverick was released on 17 April—the same day of the year that the Mustang was released.

The Maverick did well, selling more than 150,000 units in its first six months. The car's success should have told Ford and the rest of Detroit that the American public was interested in a well-built, economical car. Unfortunately, Ford's next entry in the race was the Pinto.

THE PINTO

Lee Iacocca had been working on the Pinto, Ford's first subcompact, throughout the power struggle with Bunkie Knudsen. In true Iacocca fashion he developed a new slogan— 2000:2000, a car that weighed less than 2000 pounds and cost less than $2000. At the end of 1970, the Pinto was introduced, weighing only 2030 pounds and costing less than $2000, which in those times of inflation was no small feat.

Design and production of the car took just 37 months, six months less than the typical time. What made this truly remarkable was that the Pinto was a new car in every sense of the word—new platform, new sheet metal. The Edsel, the Mustang and the Continental could trace their roots to previous models.

The Pinto seemed destined to be another shining star for Lee Iacocca. The little car sold over 250,000 units its first year on the market, but as history has revealed the Pinto is remembered not for its sales but for its notoriety.

In May 1972, as Lily Gray attempted to merge with the traffic on the freeway near her Santa Ana, California home her brand-new Pinto stalled. The car behind her couldn't stop in time and rear-ended the Pinto, rupturing the fuel tank, which was sandwiched between the rear bumper and the axle. The car exploded into flames and Lily Gray died.

Mrs Gray was not the only person to die in a flaming Pinto. According to one report, 59 people died in accidents in which a Pinto burst into flames after a rear-end collision, and many others were seriously burned. Ford was faced with hundreds of lawsuits alleging improper fuel-system design. In one major case, the company was charged with reckless homicide, and although Ford was acquitted, the negative publicity was enough to permanently imprint on the mind of the American public the image of the Pinto as a deathtrap.

Ford Motor Company admitted there were problems with the car's design. The position of the gas tank could and did lead to a fire if rear-ended. This design was not unusual. In fact, at that time *all* small cars were designed with the fuel tank located behind the axle. If a collision did occur, chances were that the light-weight

Below: *When Ford realized that the Mustang had grown too big, it tried to right a wrong with the release of the smaller Mustang II. The Mustang II enjoyed moderate success, but it could never capture the magic of its predecessor. This is a 1975 model.*

Above: *The 1975 Granada was part of Ford's plan to produce smaller cars. Weighing in at roughly 1.5 tons, the Granada was powered by either a straight-six or a V8.*

Opposite top: *Though subcompacts were much in demand throughout the 1970s, Ford's Country Squire station wagon was still the choice of many families across the United States.*

Opposite bottom: *By 1977, the Ford Thunderbird was related to the 1955 model in name only. The sexy sports car was now a luxury sedan.*

frame of any subcompact would be crushed, trapping the occupants inside.

The Pinto, however, had an additional design flaw. The filler neck on the fuel tank had a tendency to be ripped out if the car was involved in a collision. Gas would leak out, increasing the probability of a lethal explosion.

The idea for the Pinto was a good one. The public did want a small, economical car, but being a completely new car was at the heart of its problems. Although Detroit proudly introduces new cars each year, few are new from the ground up. The advantage of using an existing base is that all the glitches have been worked out. As noted earlier, the Pinto was completed in record time.

The tendency is to blame Ford management for pushing through the Pinto. Ford had in fact conducted rear-end collision tests on the Pinto during the developmental stages—and the gas tanks ruptured, but the awful significance of this was apparently ignored. However, Tom Feahheny, chief systems engineer when the

Pinto was being developed, later asserted 'If I had discovered something which was seriously wrong and which needed correction, I would not have been afraid to stand up to Lee and tell him. The truth is that, at the beginning, we just did not know.'

After the Pinto's release, Ford attempted to correct the Pinto's defects. The Pinto was lightweight because Ford had essentially cut off the rear end. It lacked the rear subframe members—the solid steel frame that forms the skeleton for the trunk and that also protects the gas tank if the car is rear-ended. Ford soon realized that the rear end of the Pinto had to be changed, so steel was added for protection. But steel adds weight, which in turn calls for a more powerful engine. The more powerful engine needs a heavier transmission. The entire car just sort of ballooned, as bigger and bigger components were added. By 1977, the Pinto weighed 2600 pounds.

The additional weight and modifications did make the Pinto safer, but it was no longer the innovative, light-weight little car that Lee Iacocca had envisioned. Of course, the 1971 to 1976 models of the Pinto were still defective, and on 15 June 1978, Ford announced it would recall 1.37 million Pintos and 30,000 Bobcats (the Mercury version of the Pinto).

To a growing segment of the American public, the Pinto typified what was wrong with the domestic auto industry. In comparison to imports, American cars were inferior. Frustrated with cars that were underpowered, lacked style—and in the case of the Pinto, were downright dangerous—consumers turned increasingly to imports.

The Pinto and the inferior quality that it had come to stand for was only part of the problem. Events that Detroit could not control were exerting their influence on the car-buying public. The ever-volatile situation in the Middle

Above and opposite bottom: *Wearing a new look for the 1970s, the Mustang still offered sports car fun at a reasonable price.*

Opposite top: *The Zephyr was Mercury's late 1970s version of the Ford Fairlane. The Mercury Cougar, the original Mustang clone, was now a cousin to the Thunderbird.*

East erupted once again in October 1973 during the Yom Kippur holy days, when Egyptian and Syrian forces attacked Israel. The Israelis proved victorious, but the Arabs retaliated by placing an embargo on petroleum exports to the West. With its supply of oil from the Mideast cut off, the United States suddenly found itself in a fuel crisis, as prices at the gas pumps soared. Service stations—at least those lucky enough to have gas—were faced with long lines and angry customers.

The oil embargo lasted five months, and when it was over, more Americans recognized the virtues of the fuel-efficient imports. In 1973, imports held a 15.3 share of the market, but by 1975 imports accounted for 15.8 percent of the market. In 1976, it seemed that Americans had forgotten the pain of the oil embargo. Detroit enjoyed a brief renaissance, while the imports' market share fell to 14.8 percent. The next year, however, the import market share reached a record high 18.5 percent, with sales of over two million cars.

In 1978 the Organization of Petroleum Exporting Countries (OPEC) prompted another fuel crisis when it raised oil prices by more than 50 percent over the next year. Then, in December 1979, five OPEC members raised prices another 13 percent. Faced with ever-increasing oil prices, Americans turned away from Detroit's gas guzzlers. In 1979, imports made up 21.8 percent of the market share. The next year the import market share had climbed to 26.7 percent, and by 1982 to a record 27.9 percent market share, as sales of imports exceeded 2.2 million cars. For the first time in 20 years, domestic automakers sold less than six million cars.

In the early 1980s, the auto industry in general was struggling to survive. Ford Motor Company was on the verge of total collapse. For three straight years, the company posted net losses totaling $3.26 billion. A number of factors contributed to Ford's decline. In addition to the challenge from imports, Ford faced stiff competition from General Motors, whose

stronger financial position allowed it to out-promote and outsell Ford (even though its products weren't necessarily any better). But a significant problem was the slipshod quality of Ford products.

At the time, public attention was directed to Chrysler's well-publicized financial crisis. After his dismissal from Ford, Lee Iacocca moved to Chrsyler and persuaded Congress and the Federal Reserve Board to guarantee a $1.2 billion loan that became known as the 'Chrysler Bailout.' The situation at Ford was almost as dismal, and some industry analysts considered it to be even worse, for the collapse of the larger Ford Motor Company would have a greater impact on the American economy.

Throughout 1980 and 1981 financial and business papers spoke of Ford's predicament in dire terms. *Business Week* in February 1981 described Ford's situation as 'rapidly deteriorating.' In April 1981 the *Los Angeles Times* declared 'The giant Ford is now on its knees.'

FORD TRUCKS

In a sense, the first Ford trucks were created, not by Ford Motor Company, but by its customers who built special bodies for their Model-Ts. In response, Ford finally started designing various vehicles to be used for hauling.

One-ton trucks first appeared in 1923 in several body types with open and closed cabs, and two years later truck buyers could choose a half-ton pickup.

During the Great Depression, Ford developed a number of truck bodies that were useful for a wide variety of purposes. The bodies were fitted to the new Model A truck chassis with four-speed transmission, dual rear wheels and a wheelbase of either 134 or 157 inches. In that era, Ford trucks did better against the competition than Ford cars did, outselling Chevrolet in 1930, 1931, 1932, 1935 and 1937. After 1937, however, Chevrolet took first place.

Ford trucks had always been a standard on the family farm, but Ford had yet to produce heavy duty trucks, a problem it corrected with the introduction of the F-7 and F-8 models in 1947. This move increased Ford's sales, but the company was still behind Chevrolet.

In 1953, as the result of engineering and customer studies, Ford introduced a new series of commercial vehicles with better lines, roomier interiors, better visibility, and better springs and steering. Though Chevrolet held onto first place, Ford's new line provided a serious challenge.

In 1957, Ford's F Series pickup trucks underwent dramatic changes. The 1956 trucks could trace their heritage all the way back to F-1s of 1948, but with the 1957 trucks, Ford was introducing something 'boldly modern,' as its advertising proclaimed. The most obvious change could be seen in the front, where the separate front fenders were replaced with thinner, slab-sided fenders that flowed back to the door. Ford also changed the hood, making it flatter and wider than previous models. Gone

Right: A beautifully restored Ford F-100 pickup truck from the mid 1950s. Strictly utilitarian vehicles in their day, trucks of this sort have now achieved classic status.

too were the exterior running boards. Instead, the designers moved the steps inside the cab, creating a smoother, more modern look.

Another innovation was the availability of two styles of pickup beds: the Styleside and the Flareside. The Styleside, which was a response to the 1955 Chevrolet Cameo, had its rear fender wheel tubs within the confines of the pickup box, while the Flareside had a narrow box flanked by two wide fenders. Truck buyers overwhelmingly preferred the Styleside to the Flareside and, unlike its Chevrolet counterpart, didn't have to pay extra for it.

Both styles were available on the F-100, the base level half-ton truck. The F-100 came in two bed lengths: a 6.5-foot box on a 110-inch wheelbase and an eight-foot box on a 118-inch

wheelbase. The F-250, a three-quarter-ton truck, was available with only an eight-foot Styleside bed. The F-350 was rated as a three-quarter-ton, but it could handle heavy duty needs up to a ton.

The public responded well to the changes Ford had made in its truck line in 1957, buying more than 265,500 trucks to give Ford a 33 percent market share.

With the arrival of the 1960s, truck buyers were becoming more sophisticated. In addition to dependability, durability and economy, they wanted trucks that were stylish, comfortable and easier to maintain. Since the late 1950s, Ford had been developing a plan for giving buyers what they wanted, and in 1961 a dramatically restyled line of trucks was unveiled.

Above: *The F-100 series was most often seen as a standard pickup truck, but was also available in other configurations, such as the delivery truck at top.*

The 1991 F-150 pickup (opposite top) has a sportier look than its 1965 counterpart (opposite bottom). Sales of pickups have increased dramatically in the last decade as consumers, men and women alike, sought practical and versatile vehicles.

The big news in 1965 was a new independent front suspension system on the F Series trucks. Called the Twin-I-Beam, the new system featured two separate I-beam forged axles that were located fore and aft by radius rods that connected to each axle half and to the frame. With each axle moving separately, this ingenious system was tough enough to withstand abuse while giving a more car-like ride.

Satisfied with the changes that it had made to the light truck line, Ford left the vehicles basically unchanged until model year 1967. As it had a decade earlier, Ford unveiled a completely redesigned line of F Series trucks, with a slab-sided cab and matching Styleside pickup box. The new ultra-modern design propelled Ford trucks into the 1970s. Indeed, the design would persist through the new decade, with revisions in 1972 and 1973.

For the first time, the cabs used curved side glass, resulting in a roomier interior. Cabs were color-coordinated, with car-like instrument panels in a padded dash. As always, the Custom Cab package offered more deluxe appointments, and if even more luxury was desired, there was the new Ranger package with a few extra amenities and lots of brightmetal trim.

Since 1981, the popularity of light trucks has grown as trucks have evolved to combine car-like features with the versatility and durability that people traditionally expect from a truck. By 1989, more consumers purchased the Ford F Series pickup than any car nameplate.

Ford's goal for the 1990s was to attract new buyers who wanted the conveniences found in a car, while still appealing to the traditional buyer. The 1991 model light trucks offered plenty of new features designed to attract new buyers. For example, there are new sport models for the F Series full-sized pickup and Ford Ranger compact pickup truck lineups.

The image leader for 1991 is the F-150 Nite, a 'street machine' with a sleek look, ample power and excellent road-handling. Power choices include a 185-hp 5.0-liter (305-ci) electronically fuel-injected (EFI) V9 or a 210 hp 5.8-liter (354-ci) EFI V8 engine. The F-150 Nite is available as a regular cab 4x2 or 4x4 model with a 117- or 133-inch wheelbase.

Only the tires, wheels, engines and transmissions on the F Series trucks were the same; everything else was revised in some way. The Styleside F-100s and F-250s had an integral cab and body arrangement, resulting in a much more stylish appearance.

Ford promoted the cab interiors as 'Driverized,' and made various modifications to improve driver comfort and convenience. The wheelbases on the F Series were lengthened, creating a better ride, longer bodies and more loadspace capacity.

Powertrains included the 223-ci (3.7-liter) Mileage Maker six as standard, a 262-ci (4.3-liter) six-cylinder and the 292-ci (4.8-liter) Y-block V8. The range of transmissions was designed to fit everyone's needs and desires: a standard three-speed All-Synchro Silent, an overdrive transmission, a heavy-duty three-speed manual, a four-speed manual and a beefed-up Cruise-O-Matic.

THE RANCHERO

In 1957, Ford Motor Company added an innovative new vehicle to its line of trucks—the Ranchero, a vehicle designed to bridge the gap between a car and a truck. Ford of Australia had been producing a similar vehicle, the Ute, since the 1930s, but to the American public, the concept of a hybrid car-truck was new and exciting.

Some people compared the Ranchero to a station wagon with the back end of the roof removed, and indeed they were closer to the truth than they realized. The Ranchero was

built on the same frame as the Ranch Wagon, Ford's base model station wagon, and used the same body, doors, engine, bumpers and interior.

The Ranchero sat on a 116-inch wheelbase and measured 203.5 inches. The base Ranchero, Model 66A, came equipped with a 223-ci (3.7-liter) overhead valve six-cylinder engine and a three-speed manual transmission with a column-mounted shifter. A 272-ci (4.5-liter) V8 was optional.

For roughly $50 more, the Custom Ranchero, Model 66B, offered even more flash, with trim on the side, a plusher interior and two-tone paint, a popular feature in the 1950s.

Over 21,700 Rancheros were sold in 1957, more than two-thirds of them the Custom model.

In 1959, the Ranchero underwent a complete restyling to compete with Chevy's new El Camino. For two years, the Ranchero had had the market to itself and Ford didn't want to lose its advantage. The new Ranchero was based on the 1959 Ford car line, a style that was more conservative than Chevrolet's wild 'bat wing.'

Ford had dropped the base line model because consumers favored the deluxe version. Moreover, the Ranchero was now based on the Ford Country Sedan station wagon, a step up from the Ranch Wagon, the previous base. In comparison to the Chevy El Camino, the Ranchero had the plusher appointments, but the El Camino offered more engine and transmission options. Though the Ranchero sold for less, more people opted for El Camino. The issue was not so much value for the dollar as brand loyalty. In 1959, Chevy people bought Chevys and Ford people bought Fords.

In 1960, Ford reversed its position and downsized the Ranchero, using the Falcon platform. Smaller, cheaper and less powerful than its previous incarnations, the Falcon Ranchero, as it was now called, proved to be a better seller than the larger versions.

Chevrolet's El Camino, in comparison, was longer and offered more power, but its strongest selling point was the Chevy name. The El Camino outsold Ford's Ranchero two to one, even though it was more expensive.

In 1966, the Ranchero again underwent major restyling, as symbolized by dropping the Falcon name. Once again, the car-truck was referred to simply as the Ranchero or the Custom Ranchero.

The exterior was smoother and more elegant, looking more like a car than a truck. The interior was roomier than before and featured a new instrument panel set in a padded dash. The optional 200 (3.3-liter) six-cylinder engine was now standard.

The Ranchero was heavier by 200 pounds and the wheelbase was increased by 3.5 inches to 113 inches. The increase in the overall size and weight gave the Ranchero a smoother, more comfortable ride. Bigger size meant a bigger price tag, but sales were good nevertheless, totalling about 22,000 units.

Built on the mid-sized Fairlane base, the Ranchero in 1967 was longer and heavier than its predecessor. Available in three levels of trim, the Ranchero had a lot to offer, even on the base model. In fact, the 1967 Ranchero offered more equipment and engine options than ever before. Consumers, however, weren't impressed and sales dropped.

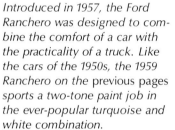

Introduced in 1957, the Ford Ranchero was designed to combine the comfort of a car with the practicality of a truck. Like the cars of the 1950s, the 1959 Ranchero on the previous pages sports a two-tone paint job in the ever-popular turquoise and white combination.

The Ranchero below is from 1971 and has the long, lean lines of the cars of that era.

THE BRONCO

In August 1965, Ford entered a new segment of the market, the sport utility segment. This kind of vehicle is smaller than a pickup, with more compact dimensions. Like Ford's Ranchero, a sports utility vehicle combines attributes of both cars and trucks to fill a variety of purposes. At that time, there were only two manufacturers—International Harvester and Kaiser Jeep, makers of, respectively, Scout and Jeep. Combined annual sales totaled only 35,000. However, Ford believed that this market would grow, and decided to introduce its own sports vehicle—the 1966 Ford Bronco.

The new Ford Bronco was smaller and more compact than the F-100 truck or the Falcon Ranchero. Like the Scout and Jeep, it had a boxy shape and was available in three body styles: a four-passenger wagon with a removable full-length roof, a pickup with a half roof and an open-top, two-door roadster with a choice of two- or four-passenger seating.

Ford wanted to tie the Bronco in with the Mustang, which was at the height of its popularity in 1966, and declared that both 'were designed for the same type of people... modern, active Americans on the go.' After conducting extensive market research, Ford concluded that consumers wanted comfortable seats, protection from the elements and reliable parts and service. In addition, consumers were interested in a vehicle with a short turning radius and the ability to climb steep grades and maintain highway speeds. The public got exactly what it asked for. The Bronco was peppy, fun to drive and equally at home on the highway or off. In its first year, Bronco had sales of 18,200.

The original drivetrain was a 170-ci (2.8-liter), 104-hp in-line six-cylinder with a fully synchronized three-speed manual transmission, full-time four-wheel-drive and a solid front driving axle. The wheelbase was an easy-to-handle 92 inches and the overall length was 152.1 inches.

In March 1966, Ford's small-block V8 became available in the 289-ci (4.7-liter) and two years later in the 302-ci (5.0-liter). By 1973 only the wagon version of the Bronco remained. With the exception of refinements to improve performance, handling and appearance, the Bronco existed in its basic form for over a decade. Then, in the 1978 model year, the Bronco became a full-sized (104.7-inch) utility vehicle. The new Bronco had seating for six, a removable fiberglass rear roof and a more car-like interior. Power choices included the two big V8s, a 351-ci (5.8-liter) and a 400-ci (6.6-liter).

The Bronco would remain basically unchanged until 1987, when the front end was restyled with a new fender and hood sheet metal, new aero-style wraparound impact-resistant headlights and directional signals and a larger front bumper. Ride and handling were improved with the addition of gas-pressurized shock absorbers and adjustable caster and camber as standard equipment. The 'Touch Drive' system, which provides in-cab shift-on-the-fly capabilities for the 4x4, was offered as an option.

Since its introduction in 1966, the Bronco has been known as a go-anywhere, do-anything vehicle. Almost immediately it became a favorite with off-road performance buffs.

To celebrate 25 years of enduring popularity, Ford offered a Silver Anniversary Edition of the Bronco in 1991. Only 3000 units of the Silver Anniversary package were built. The special edition Bronco featured a currant red exterior with matching fiberglass roof. An emblem designating the Silver Anniversary appears on the front fender, instrument panel and front floor mats.

When Ford unveiled its Bronco in 1966 (at top), there were only two other manufacturers of sports utility vehicles. By the time the Bronco celebrated its 25th anniversary in 1991 (above), virtually every car maker offered a similar vehicle.

The standard powertrain for the Silver Anniversary Bronco is a 5.0-liter (305-ci) electronically fuel injected (EFI) V8 with electronic automatic overdrive transmission.

THE EXPLORER

In March 1990, Ford introduced the 1991 Explorer, a new entry in the compact utility vehicle market. Since its release, the Explorer has proven to be a popular combination of car and truck conveniences. As Thomas Wagner, Ford Division general manager, explained, 'Explorer looks more truck-like than car-like,

Above: Trucks undergo testing at Ford's Arizona Proving Ground. Covering 3840 acres of mountainous terrain, the proving ground contains a five mile oval high speed track, wet traction test surfaces and various concrete and gravel roads for performance and durability testing.

yet it offers some of the same comforts you would expect to find in cars—right down to the lighted vanity mirrors, the optional compact disc player and leather seats.' On the other hand, Explorer has its share of truck attributes: part-time four-wheel-drive, trailer towing, plenty of cargo space and a heavy-duty frame and suspension.

The Explorer line-up includes two- and four-door and two-wheel and four-wheel-drive models. The four-door models, which can seat up to six passengers, are targeted at families, while the more compact two-door model is suited to the single buyer looking for an easy to maneuver, versatile vehicle.

Ford notes that the Explorer appeals to women, particularly for urban driving because it has a number of safety features, such as child-proof rear locks and excellent handling in adverse weather conditions.

The 1991 Explorer features a 4.0-liter (244-ci) V6 engine that generates 155 hp at 4200 rpm and 220 foot pounds of torque at 2400 rpm. The engine is teamed with a standard five-speed manual overdrive or optional four-speed automatic overdrive transmission.

Previous pages: The Aeromax L-9000, the flagship of Ford's heavy duty line of trucks.

THE AEROSTAR

Like the Ford Explorer, the Aerostar minivan has experienced a recent surge in popularity as Americans look for a vehicle that can take the kids, operate as a commuter car and accommodate the entire family for a weekend getaway.

The Ford Aerostar offers the security of four-wheel-drive and trailer-towing capabilities. Both functional and sporty, the Aerostar features an attractive interior and plenty of storage space with fishnet cargo covers, as well as many outstanding configurations and options.

HEAVY-DUTY TRUCKS

After half a century as one of the leading automobile and light truck manufacturers in the United States, Ford entered into the heavy truck market in the late 1960s with its Louisville line of cabs.

Today, Ford, like the rest of the major truck manufacturers, is responding to the trucking industry's demand for state-of-the-art aerodynamics with the introduction of its AeroForce line—the AeroMax, the newest Ford heavy truck, and the LTL-9000, CLT-9000 and L-9000 Series, all equipped with an aerodynamics package that includes roof reinforcements, roof fairings, cab side extenders and an adjustable top panel. Extensive wind-tunnel testing, full-size vehicle coastdown work on test tracks and real-world fleet tests went into the development of the AeroForce fleet. In the summer of 1987, Ford put the LTL and CL to the test in a 3500-mile road run from Anaheim to Philadelphia—through California's rugged Donner Pass, and over the Rockies. Powered by a Cummins L-10, the CL-9000 averaged 8.27 mpg and the LTL-9000 averaged 6.58 mpg.

Ford added the Caterpillar 3306B Standard and Economy models at 285 and 300 hp to the list of options in 1989. The 3306B weighs about 800 pounds less than the 3406B, and that reduction means greater payloads. The lightweight Cummins L-10 is standard—out of a choice of 28 Cummins or Caterpillar engines. For more power, there's the Big Cam IV (OAC) Series, which includes the Formula with up to 400 hp and the NTC with up to 444 hp. The NTC 444 gets high marks with truckers because it is durable, moves well from a cold start, and has a standard compression brake.

THE AEROMAX

The flagship of the Ford AeroForce is the AeroMax. Introduced in 1988, it is the most fuel-efficient conventional in the fleet. The design of the AeroMax directs air over the top and, more importantly, around a vehicle. Even the headlights and turn signals are built flush to improve air flow around the fenders. Fuel tank fairings and a cab valance panel close the gap over the fuel tanks and between the cab for reduced drag. Ford reports that the AeroMax averages 7.88 mpg.

As Ford points out, 'Getting to an inner-city destination on time is one thing. Getting around tight loading docks and narrow city streets is another.' Thanks to a set-back front axle and 53-foot turning diameter, the AeroMax maneuvers well. The set-back front axle design also contributes to effective weight distribution since more payload can be transferred to the front axle.

For comfort, the Ford AeroForce offers a choice of 16 seats, including Cush-N-Aire, a favorite among those who log thousands of miles a year. The instrument panel features aircraft-type back lights and pointers for easy reading. The gauges are set to indicate 'normal' when the pointers are at 3:00. That means a quick glance is all that's needed for a systems check.

One of the AeroMax's nicest features is the sleeper, which includes air conditioning, two radio speakers, a lighted luggage compartment and a digital alarm clock. But probably the best option is the 12-volt DC refrigerator—for those times when you're tired of truck stop fare or are in the mood for a midnight snack.

LTL-9000

Ford calls the LTL-9000 conventional a 'proven performer.'
In July 1987, an AeroForce LTL, powered by a Caterpillar 3406B economy diesel, was tested in a 1765-mile fleet run from Ohio to Texas against a non-Aeroforce 1985 LTL-9000. The new LTL got 7.35 mpg, compared to 6.29 mpg for the old. That represents a 17 percent improvement.

By setting components like fuel tanks, air tanks and battery boxes under the cab, the LTL-9000 is able to load enough weight onto the front axle for high payload capacity. The single axle LL-9000 is ideal for big volume, low weight applications, such as bulk-mail delivery.

It may not be the Ritz, but the 60-inch Penthouse Sleeper does offer first class accommodations while on the road. For truckers who need to be orderly and organized, the Penthouse features a full-length closet, two luggage compartments, a three-drawer dresser and two under-bunk storage drawers.

Below: *The Ford Aerostar minivan is popular among young, growing families.*

At bottom: *The Explorer is also popular with families. New in 1991, the Explorer is an updated version of the Bronco II.*

CLT-9000

Ford's CLT-9000 ranks among the leaders in aerodynamic cabover design. Everything about this truck—-from the sloped windshield to the recessed steps and grab handles—-is designed to cut drag and improve mileage. Averaging 8.27 miles per gallon, this is the most fuel-efficient truck in the AeroForce Fleet.

Like the rest of the fleet, the CLT-9000 can be spec'd with a Fuller nine-speed overdrive RTX transmission. Some truckers like the RTX because the 'H' shift pattern is simpler to use, as well as more economical, than 10- and 13-speed transmissions. Other transmission options on the CLT-9000 run the gamut from a seven-speed Spicer to a 13-speed Fuller. The CLT also has the same choice of engines as the other AeroForce trucks, from the standard L-10 at 240 hp to the powerful NTC at 444 hp.

This AeroForce cabover has one of the smoothest rides around. The four-point air-ride suspension really does isolate the driver from chassis noise and vibration. For added comfort, options for the rear suspension include HA-360 and HA-400, rated at 36,000 and 40,000 pounds, respectively.

Since the truck itself is part of the trucker's identity, Ford believes in giving truckers lots of options. Besides the choice of engines, truckers can select paints, trims and seats, as well as modify the cab and chassis. For starters,

Ford offers a choice of 16 colors—-from Wild Strawberry to Bahama Blue—-on the cab and another six colors on the frame. Some sparkle can be added with a bright grille, muffler, stack and elbow and an aluminum bumper. Dietz roof marker lights and dual Hadley air horns provide the finishing touches.

L-9000 SERIES

The 9000 Series is a successor to the Louisville Line cabs, introduced 20 years ago. The AeroForce L-9000 Series consists of the conventional L/LT-9000, the set-back LS/LTS-9000 and the short-nose LN/LNT. With a variety of configurations plus GCWRs up to 138,000 pounds, the L-9000 Series covers a broad range of line-haul applications. The LS-9000 has a set-back front axle for better maneuverability, and the resulting short wheelbase transfers more payload to the front axle.

THE WORKFORCE

As part of Ford's 'Work-Ready Program,' the L-9000 Series, the LL/LTL-9000 and the CL/CLT-9000 are ready to meet the specific requirements of a given job—construction, refuse and so on. The frame, powertrain and suspension/axle capabilities are pre-spec'd to fit the truck to the job. For example, the CLT can be tailored for municipal needs or the LTL-9000 for flatbed logging.

Opposite top: *A Ford LTL-9000 on the job site.*

Opposite bottom: *The aerodynamic design of the Ford CLT-9000 has made it one of the best cabovers in the industry.*

Above: *A successor to the Louisville line of cabs, the L-9000 features a set-back front axle for better maneuverability.*

'QUALITY IS JOB ONE'

Facing page: *The 1982 LTD Crown Victoria. Though many people in the 1980s opted for smaller imports, some segments of the market still preferred the classic lines of an American sedan.*

Ford's plan was to give the people what they wanted. It would continue to make cars for those people who had remained faithful to the archetypal Detroit auto, but Ford would also attempt to woo the consumers who wanted fuel efficient, streamlined designs.

While the press was reporting Ford's decline, the company, under the guidance of its new chief executive officer, Philip Caldwell, was planning its strategy for survival. Caldwell's first step was to cut costs. Between 1979 and 1980, Ford reduced its work force by 60,000, and the following year an additional 9000 employees were laid off. The 1980 production schedule was cut by 250,000 cars. If fewer cars were built, payroll costs would be lower. The layoffs affected all Ford personnel, not just the hourly production workers. 'Ongoing automotive-related salaried positions' were cut by 44,000 jobs between 1979 and 1981, and a half a dozen plants were closed over a four-year period.

Caldwell's cost-cutting program proved effective. In an 18-month period beginning in 1980, roughly $2.5 billion was shaved from fixed costs, and an additional $500 million was cut the next year. Caldwell regretted that the cost-production program led to so many people losing their jobs, explaining 'It meant doing a lot of things we would much rather have avoided, because human beings were involved. But we had to do it to survive.'

Cost-cutting measures are only temporary solutions. At the heart of the problem was the fact that consumers had lost trust in the Ford name. Caldwell recognized that American consumers, having first turned to imports because they were fuel efficient, were now buying European and Japanese cars because they appreciated the overall quality of the product. As he was preparing for a meeting with top management, Caldwell jotted down the words 'quality—number one' and thus was born a new slogan—'Quality is job one'—and, more importantly, a new philosophy. In car-making jargon, *job one* stands for the first car of a new model as it starts down the assembly line. With its new slogan, Ford was asserting that *quality* would be the first element that went into every single car it made.

Caldwell envisioned Ford Motor Company as a domestic and world leader in automotive styling, engineering, construction and durability. Obviously, such a bold assertion required drastic measures, enormous risks and money. Ford would have to change the adversarial relationship that existed between management and labor, production facilities needed to be updated with the latest technological advances to improve efficiency and productivity and, above all, Ford cars had to be better than all the other cars that Detroit had to offer. 'They were to be drivers' cars—functional, comfortable, good-looking and distinctive,' declared Caldwell.

During his tenure at Ford of Europe, Caldwell had developed an appreciation for the rounder, more aerodynamic styling of European cars. From the very beginning of the auto industry, European drivers had had different needs than their counterparts in the United States. Until recent years, Americans were unconcerned about the supply of oil and consequently built big, boxy cars that had terrible gas mileage. Europeans, however, were never oil rich and gasoline was expensive. Thus, cars were designed to be as fuel efficient as possible, which involved the engineering of the motor and the drivetrain as well as the overall size and styling. In general, European cars were smaller, lighter and more streamlined than those built in America. Ford of Europe had adapted European styling for the cars it produced for the international market, and now the time had come for the European influence to make its way across the Atlantic. Jack

Telnack, the head of the design shop at Ford of Europe in the 1970s, was back in Detroit. When the word came down from the top, Telnack and his team of designers were eager to work on aerodynamic styling.

In 1983, Ford released its first aerodynamically styled cars. In February the Ford Thunderbird and its cousin, the Mercury Cougar, were unveiled, looking very different from the previous models. Gone was the traditional boxy look, and in its place was the aeroshape—which some critics likened to an eggshell. The new Ford Tempo and Mercury Topaz, introduced in May, also had aerodynamic styling, as did the Lincoln Continental Mark VII, which was released that fall.

The styling modifications of these cars represented only the tip of the iceberg. Since 1979, Ford had been developing a totally new and different car with aerodynamic styling. Though the public had accepted the aeroshape on the Thunderbird, Cougar and Mark VII, they were specialty cars and could afford to be a bit different. Ford was proposing to challenge the American concept of what a mid-sized family car should look like.

Caldwell had asked the development team to estimate the cost of developing an entirely new family of cars, from concept to the show-room. The estimate was $3.1 billion, but that didn't include modernizing plants and making various engineering improvements. To cover those costs, $2 billion more was needed. While $5.1 billion sounds like a phenomenal amount to develop a new car, what it really stood for was competing with GM and the import market. Many of the members of Ford's board of directors were reluctant to commit what amounted to half of the company's net worth, but Caldwell and his key executives convinced them that Ford had no choice but to take the risk. The board gave their approval, and the Ford Taurus/Mercury Sable program was underway.

In its earliest stages of development, the Taurus project was truly a team effort. It represented a change from the old hierarchy with a central, dominant figure calling all the shots.

In contrast to the involved procedures Ford had used to name its cars, such as the Edsel or the Thunderbird, the Taurus name evolved much more simply. While chatting one day, Lewis Veraldi and John W Risk, the planning director, discovered that both of their wives were born under the astrological sign of Taurus. The company tested public reaction to the name and received a positive response, and Ford liked the imagery the name evoked.

Below: The mark of success— the 1980 Lincoln Mark VI. The Mark has consistently been one of Ford's biggest money makers.

According to astrological lore, people born under the sign of Taurus are practical, determined and deliberate—admirable qualities for a family car. Moreover, the sign of the bull seemed an appropriate symbol for a car that must have the strength and brute force necessary to save the company from financial disaster.

Sable, on the other hand, was meant to convey a sleek, classy image. The two cars are almost identical mechanically, but the Mercury Sable has a sleeker exterior and a more elegant interior. In essence, the Sable is a sportier car with more pizzazz, designed to appeal to younger buyers, while the Taurus, a heavier, more subdued car, is directed toward the middle-aged, family person.

Market research has long been a part of developing a new car, but automakers didn't necessarily pay attention to what customers wanted. With the Taurus, Ford was committed to giving people what they wanted. They research team *was* an integral part of the Taurus team and did effect the final product. In April 1981, the size of the car was changed. When the Taurus was first being planned, the nation was still reeling from the effects of the

oil crisis of the 1970s. Gas prices were climbing and consumers were interested in small, fuel-efficient automobiles. Five years down the road, which is when the Taurus would be released, the market would have different demands. When oil prices started to fall, research indicated that the public would again favor larger, more impressive cars. Given that assessment, the Taurus team went back to the drawing board and enlarged the wheelbase, widened the track and increased the overall volume.

Market research also revealed an interesting fact about how the public perceived Ford. Management was concerned that the American public was angry with the Ford Motor Company for bringing an American institution to the brink of failure. The truth was that people didn't care. Ford was horrified to discover that Americans were indifferent to an American legend.

Armed with this disconcerting bit of information, Ford stopped worrying about promoting a tradition or patriotism, for in the public's eye, the company no longer represented these noble qualities. Instead, Ford concentrated on giving customers what they wanted—satisfac-

Above: *Though its mission has varied through the years, the Ford Thunderbird has never been short on appeal. This is a 1980 model.*

Above: *Throughout the 1980s, the Ford Escort was one of the best-selling cars in America. Priced right and promising excellent gas mileage, the Escort was snapped up in record numbers around the United States.*

Opposite top: *The final assembly line at Ford's Wayne, Michigan plant. In a process called engine decking, the Escort body hovers over a machine that places the engine in the front-wheel drive car. With rear-wheel drive cars, the engines are dropped into their compartments from overhead.*

Opposite bottom: *Ford's V8 powered Mustang GT convertible for 1985.*

tion. if Ford could produce a good car at the right price and provide reliable service, then people would buy it.

Even though there was some concern over how the public would react to the radical new aeroshape, the wind resistance, or drag, is lessened. Wind resistance is measured as the 'coefficient-of-drag' or cd, and the lower the number the better. The typical American-made car of the early 1980s had a cd of .48. European cars, with their aerodynamic styling, had much lower cds. Mercedes-Benz and Audi 5000 rated .33 cd and .32 cd, respectively.

Ford's goal was to achieve a cd rating equal to that of the best European sedans—and Ford succeeded. When the cars were released in December 1985, the Sable rated .32 and the Taurus .33. The station wagon models rated .34.

In addition to aerodynamics, Team Taurus was concerned with ergonomics—the science of relationships between humans and machines. The team studied every imaginable way a driver interacts with a car. The cockpit was designed with a slightly concave dash-board and instrument panel that brought all the controls within full view and easy reach of the driver. The seats were offered in a number

of different configurations to accommodate as many human sizes and shapes as possible. Ford's research revealed that people are often irritated by the release lever that moves the seat because they have to grope to find the lever. Ford's solution was to put a long bar just under the entire length of the front seat in easy reach of the driver.

Extensive study of the driver's and passengers' comfort yielded such features as front and side visors, a 20-inch recessed wiper blades, an electric windshield de-icer system, a left footrest, a large accelerator pedal and rope netting in the trunk so that grocery bags wouldn't fall over.

The Taurus was the subject of more product planning and research than any other car in the history of Detroit automaking. For five years, consumers were polled, interviewed and consulted about the car as it developed. Ford began surveying consumers about four-wheel drive even before the preliminary sketches of were done. Customers previewed photographs of clay models and, later, interior and exterior fiberglass mock-ups of the car. In 1984, Ford held ride-and-drive clinics, and six months before the car's December 1985 release, the company conducted a unique test-

Previous pages: *The 1983 Thun-*
derbird was the first Ford to fea-
ture the new aerodynamic
styling—and the public greeted
the change with enthusiasm.
Note the much rounder shape
on this model in comparison car
to the 1980 Thunderbird on
page 167.

Below: *The 1985 Lincoln Mark*
VII below shows the benefit of
its aerodynamic styling, whereas
the 1982 Lincoln on the right and
the Ford LTD on the far right
conform to the more traditional
look.

driving program in collaboration with Hertz Rent-a-Car. In six test markets—New York, Chicago, Atlanta, Denver, San Francisco and Los Angeles—prominent citizens received personal letters from vice presidents inviting them to free use of a Taurus for a few days. Hertz dropped off the car, filled with gas, and picked it up later. The drivers were asked to fill out a questionnaire about the car and were guaranteed that they would not be solicited by Ford dealers later on.

Team Taurus listened to the consumers' suggestions. One issue that came up concerned the lack of footroom in the back seat. Consumers noted that they had to stick their feet under the front seat and ended up scuffing their shoes on the metal seat-adjustment tracks. Ford responded by sloping the floor beneath the front seats, widening the space between the tracks and using plastic for the tracks instead of metal.

Opposite top: *More research went into the development of the Ford Taurus than any other car to come out of Detroit up to that point. Its aerodynamic styling revolutionized the American auto industry.*

Below: *The Mercury Sable was designed as a sleeker, more elegant cousin of the Ford Taurus.*

Opposite bottom: *Launched in May 1983, the Ford Tempo borrowed a few features from the Taurus. The Tempo is one of Ford's top-selling mid-priced cars today.*

The Taurus and Sable were finally released on 26 December 1985, following a full year of publicity heralding its arrival. In January 1985, Ford previewed the cars at a Hollywood gala at MGM studios attended by celebrities, reporters, columnists, editors and broadcasters. Ford unveiled the cars to the general public at the annual Chicago Auto Show. The unveiling was covered by the local media, including super station WGN, which is broadcast in 40 states via cable. Detroit and Canadian news services, as well as the CBS Evening News, all carried stories on Ford's new cars.

One of the more innovative techniques that Ford used to bring the Taurus to the attention of the public was the 'caravan' tour. Two moving vans loaded with working prototypes of the Taurus and Sable crisscrossed the country stopping at Ford facilities and plants in both big cities and small towns.

A year after its release the Taurus was the best-selling mid-sized car in America, making it Ford's most successful new model since the Mustang in 1964. In 1986, Taurus received *Motor Trend*'s Car of the Year award, in 1988 it made *Road and Track*'s list of the Best Cars in the World, and in 1989 *Car and Driver* ranked Taurus among its 'Ten Best' cars. The Industrial Designers Society of America (IDSA) recently named Taurus one of the 10 most important designs of the decade. Notably, Taurus was the *only* automobile to be included on the list.

Ford's big gamble on the Taurus paid off. The Taurus revolutionized worldwide auto design. In 1986, Ford had a 18.2 percent share of the domestic car market, up from a low of 16.6 in 1981. By 1989, its market share had climbed to 24.6 percent.

The Taurus was the crucial element in Ford's revitalization, but the Taurus represented more than a car—it was symbolic of Ford's new philosophy. Ford's goal was to meet the market's needs with quality products. While this seems to be a fairly simple and logical approach, in recent years Detroit had had a tendency to ignore this basic precept.

FORD CARS TODAY

The Ford Escort quickly dominated the domestic subcompact market when it was introduced in 1980. More than three million Escorts were sold in the first decade of its release, and sales worldwide exceed seven million. After a decade as the nation's best-selling car, the Escort was redesigned in 1991 to give it a fresher, more contemporary design. *Motor Trend* declared 'This is one domestic sedan that can play with the likes of Honda's Civic or Toyota's Corolla. *Automobile Magazine* called the Escort 'a first-class compact that can go head-to-head with its Japanese competition.'

The 1991 Escort is available in three body styles: two-door hatchback, four-door hatchback and four-door wagon. Redesigned with a lower cowl and belt to provide more glass area and visibility, the Escort's aerodynamic shape and semi-flush glass reduced the drag coefficient from .39 to .34. Other new features include flip-out quarter windows on two-door hatchback models, a remote-control outside mirror and an 'A' pillar-mounted antenna.

The interior of the 1991 Escort has seating for five and was redesigned to provide more shoulder and hip room. Using ergonomics, Ford designed a wraparound instrument panel to make driving easier.

All new front and rear suspensions provide significant improvements in ride, handling and steering, while cutting down on noise and vibration. Like the Taurus, the 1991 Escort has a powertrain subframe. Powertrain changes include the addition of sequential fuel injection to the 1.9-liter (116-ci) engine. The GT is equipped with an all new, high performance 1.8-liter (110-ci), 16-valve twin-cam engine. The powerplant produces 127 hp at 6500 rpm, delivering exceptional performance for a subcompact. The Mercury Tracer, the Escort's cousin, is available in three models: a standard four-door notchback, a station wagon and the LTS, a sporty four-door. Among Tracer's standard features are four-wheel independent suspension, tinted glass, AM/FM stereo radio, two-speed windshield wipers with fixed intervals, split-fold rear seats, reclining front seats and rear seat heat ducts.

According to Ross H Roberts, general manager of Lincoln-Mercury, the Tracer has 'a level of standard and optional equipment uncommon in this class of car. We're confident it will compare favorably with any car in its class built anywhere in the world.'

Ford Division's lowest-priced and most fuel-efficient car is the Festiva. Ford describes the four-passenger, two-door Festiva as a 'mini-car'—an apt description for a car with a wheelbase of only 90.2 inches. The car's standard 1.3-liter (79-ci), four-cylinder engine is offered with a five-speed manual or a three-speed automatic transaxle. The Festiva's excellent mileage (up to 43 miles per gallon) appeals to the entry-level buyer, a market in which the car has done reasonably well. Over 200,000 Festivas were sold in the three years following its 1987 release.

The Tempo, one of the first Ford cars to feature aerodynamic styling, has had a steady following since its introduction in May 1983. 'Tempo's strong suit has always been the value

Below: The Festiva is Ford's lowest-priced, most fuel efficient car. With a wheelbase just over 90 inches, it is also the smallest car Ford produces.

it offers for the dollar,' maintains Thomas J Wagner, Ford Division general manager. One of Tempo's unique features is four-wheel drive that can be activated at the touch of a switch, even while the car is in motion.

In 1991, the Tempo underwent a number of functional improvements designed to reduce the amount of noise, vibration and harshness experienced by the driver and passengers. Emphasizing its function as a family car, standard equipment on the 1991 Tempo includes a number of safety features, such as the manual rear lap/shoulder safety belts and a single-level emergency belt release for the front seat automatic shoulder belt. Air bags on the driver's side are optional.

The Mercury Topaz underwent similar refinements on its 1991 model, receiving an upgraded sound package to reduce interior noise. The Topaz is offered in four different series: the two- and four-door GS, four-door LS and LTS and the sporty XR5 two-door. The GS and LS are powered by a 2.3-liter (140-ci) electronic fuel injection High Swirl Combustion (HSC) four-cylinder engine coupled with a five-speed manual transaxle, or an optional three-speed automatic transaxle.

LUXURY SEDANS

The big, classy cars that fell into disfavor with the oil crisis enjoyed a renaissance in the late 1980s. Between 1979 and 1982, automakers were downsizing their cars and converting them to front-wheel drive. With a huge outlay of cash committed to the Taurus program, Ford simply couldn't afford to downsize its entire line, so it left the Lincoln Town Car, the Ford Crown Victoria and the Mercury Marquis as they were and made plans to phase them out. The tide turned in Ford's favor, however, when the oil crisis passed and conservative drivers once again sought large, luxurious cars. GM had downsized its autos, and sales of the downsized Cadillac Eldorados and Sevilles dropped off considerably as buyers turned to the luxury cars of Ford/Lincoln-Mercury.

Today, the Crown Victoria and Mercury Marquis are some of the few cars still using body-on-frame construction. They appeared on their current platform in 1978, underwent a facelift in 1988 and received a restyled exterior in 1991.

One of the roomier cars on the road, the Crown Victoria is equipped with a 5.0-liter (305-ci) V8 engine with an automatic overdrive

Above: *The best-selling Ford Escort was completely redesigned in 1991. Involving a total investment of $1.9 billion, the Ford Escort/Mercury Tracer redesign was Ford's biggest program since the launch of the Taurus in 1986.*

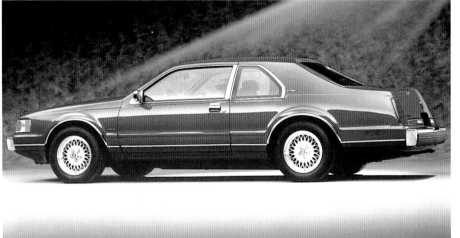

A sampling of Lincoln-Mercury's finest for 1991: the Lincoln Mark VII (above), the Mercury Sable (at top), the Mercury Cougar (opposite top) and the Lincoln Town Car (opposite bottom).

transmission. The car is available in five series—LTD Crown Victoria S (four-door sedan), LTD Crown Victoria and LTD Crown Victoria LX (four-door sedan and wagon), LTD Country Squire wagon and LTD Country Squire LX wagon. Numerous amenities, such as air conditioning, tinted glass, dual electric remote-control mirrors and side window demisters are standard on the Crown Vic.

The 1991 Crown Victoria offers a number of exterior styling refinements, such as clearcoat paint, which is designed to add luster as well as protection. In addition, the paint stripe locations are lower and brighter, and clear front park/turn lenses with amber bulbs replace the car's amber lenses. New in 1991 is a driver's side air bag.

The Mercury Grand Marquis, one of Lincoln-Mercury's best-selling models, is available in two sedan models, the GS and the LS, and two station wagons, the Colony Park GS and Colony Park LS. Like the Crown Victoria, the Grand Marquis features an improved exterior for 1991, with such touches as blacked-out paint treatment for the front grille, bright 'sparkle' treatment on the aluminum wheels, a relocated paint stripe and a new carriage roof option.

Reflecting the public's renewed interest in luxury cars, *Motor Trend* named the Lincoln Town Car Car of the Year in 1990, the first time in 38 years that a luxury sedan has been honored. In 1991, the Town Car was equipped with an all-new 4.6-liter (280-ci) V8 engine as standard. The new engine is part of a new line that Ford will use in various Ford and Lincoln-Mercury cars in the 1990s.

For over 20 years, the Lincoln Mark VII has remained a favorite with drivers who want an elegant automobile. The Mark is powered by a 225-hp, 5.0-liter (305-ci) High Output (HO) Sequential Electronic Fuel Injection (SEFI) V8 engine with a four-speed automatic overdrive transmission. The engine's high level of performance complements the car's luxury appointments.

The Mark VII is available in two models: the Bill Blass Designer Series and the Luxury Sports Coupe (LSC). Upgrades in 1991 for the Bill Blass Designer Series include a 3.27 rear axle ratio, constant-rate steering, handling suspension and BBS road wheels with a unique center inset.

The philosophy that developed the Ford Taurus was extended to Ford's other cars, including some in the luxury line. The 1988 Lincoln Continental, for example, was designed by a team, with input from line workers and suppliers. Built on the Taurus platform, the Continental benefitted from methods and technology that were developed by Team Taurus. Like the Taurus, the Continental was introduced to the public through a caravan tour. Released on 26 December 1987, the Continental was sold out by June 1988. With its release, *Car and Driver* magazine proclaimed 'The new Continental will change the way the world thinks of the American car.'

In 1991, Ford improved the powertrain with a more fuel-efficient electronic four-speed automatic transaxle. Performance was enhanced by 15 hp with engine refinements and a standard dual exhaust. As befits a luxury car, the 1991 Continental offered such options as a cellular telephone, an anti-theft alarm system and a disc player.

Though the Thunderbird today is a far cry from the two-seater that was introduced in

Below: *In 1988, the Taurus line was enhanced with an SHO (Super High Output) model.*

Opposite top: *The Grand Marquis, one of Mercury's perennial best-selling models, received an updated exterior for 1991.*

Opposite bottom: *One of the roomiest cars on the road—the 1992 Ford Crown Victoria.*

The Mercury Tracer wagon (below) and the LTS (bottom) for 1991. Both have the distinctive aero-shape.

Opposite top: Mercury resurrected the Capri name for this sporty 2 + 2.

Opposite bottom: After 25 years, the Mustang is still America's favorite 'pony car.'

1955, Ford believes that throughout its various incarnations the Thunderbird has remained a 'driver's car.' When Ford modified the Thunderbird and Cougar in 1983, the company was apprehensive about how the public would respond to the new aeroshape. Public response was positive to the changes, and in 1989 the Thunderbird was again redesigned. Once again the public was pleased with the new look, which industry analysts compared to the BMW 635 coupe. *Motor Trend* magazine named it the 1989 Car of the Year. In 1991, the Thunderbird underwent a facelift, with major upgrades to the interiors and an optional 5.0-liter (305-ci), 200 hp V8 engine.

The 1991 Mercury Cougar also received a facelift, which included revised bodyside moldings, a new grille and updated fascia, hood, headlamps and taillamps. Under the hood, the Cougar XR7 gets the same powerful 5.0-liter (302-ci) sequential electronic fuel injection (SEFI) HO V8 engine that is available on the Thunderbird.

SPORTS CARS

The Mustang—America's original 'Pony car'—celebrated its 25th anniversary in 1989. A perennial favorite among performance enthusiasts, the Mustang GT 5.0-liter (302-ci) engine was listed as one of *Motor Trend's* Top Ten performance cars (where cost is an object). In 1988, the GT was selected by *Road & Track* editors as one of the Ten Best Cars in the World based on value, and *Car and Driver* also ranked the GT on its list of 10 best cars.

The 1991 Mustang is available in three series—Mustang LX (two-door sedan, two-door hatchback and two-door convertible), 5.0-liter (302-ci) Mustang LX and Mustang GT (two-door hatchback and convertible).

In 1991, Ford improved the performance, fuel economy and driveability of the Mustang. With a new twin-plug version of Ford's 2.3-liter (140-ci) engine, performance is heightened and horsepower upped from 86 to 105. The 5.0-liter (305-ci) V8 on the GT puts out 225 hp at 4200 rpm.

The Mustang comes equipped with a high level of standard equipment, including flush, aerodynamic halogen headlamps; wraparound taillamps; dual remote-control mirrors; and color-coordinated bodyside paint stripe. In the interest of safety, a driver side airbag supplemental restraint system and rear-passenger lap/shoulder belts are standard. Options include 14-inch styled road wheels or 15-inch cast aluminum wheels with P205/65R BSW tires for the 2.3-liter (140-ci) LX, graphic equalizer and front floor mats.

Above: *Since its introduction as a 1989 model, the Probe has won accolades for its performance.* Car and Driver *named it one of its 'Ten Best' cars for 1989, and* Autoweek *included Probe its list of 'The Best and Brightest' 1989 cars.*

Opposite top: *The Thunderbird was new from the ground up in 1989. Its new platform gave the car a longer, wider stance, with a wheelbase nine inches longer than the 1988 model.*

Opposite bottom: *The Mustang GT for 1991.*

Having rebounded in its own arena, Ford decided to tackle markets that are dominated by foreign cars. The Probe, introduced in May 1988, is targeted at the small specialty market, a group that favors German and Japanese cars, and has done well against the competition. A month after the Probe was released, dealers had back orders exceeding 100,000. Buyers are primarily young, well-educated, in the middle to upper-middle income brackets and, more often than not, women.

Interestingly enough, the Probe is exported to Japan, where Ford is the number one foreign carmaker.

Brought to the United States through the Lincoln Mercury Division, the Scorpio was Ford of Europe's entry into the high performance sports sedan market. Designed to compete with Mercedes-Benz, BMW, Audi, Saab and Volvo, the Scorpio beat the European carmakers at their own game, winning numerous awards, including the 1986 Car of the Year for Europe.

The Mercury Capri is another car designed to appeal to young professionals. Introduced

in Australia in late 1989, the sporty Capri arrived in the United States in 1990. The car reflects a global effort. Ford's Ghia Studios in Italy styled the exterior, while the interior design was done by Italdesign SpA of Turin, Italy. The powertrain and chassis were developed in conjunction with Mazda, in which Ford has a 25 percent interest.

'The Capri is designed to be a fun-to-drive car—a funabout—but we didn't forget value and versatility,' explained Ross H Roberts, Ford vice president and Lincoln-Mercury general manager. A two-door convertible with 2+2 seating, the Capri is equipped with front-wheel-drive and a 1.6-liter (98-ci), double overhead cam engine with either a five-speed manual or an optional four-speed electronic automatic transmission. A removable hard top is optional. The Capri is available in two series: Capri and XR2. Standard features include power steering, power four-wheel disc brakes, tinted glass, dual remote power mirrors, power windows, electronic AM/FM stereo radio, variable intermittent windshield wipers, digital clock and leather-wrapped steering wheel.

FORD IN THE NINETIES

The 1980s saw several changes in the hierarchy of Ford's top management. In October 1982, Philip Caldwell succeeded Henry Ford II as Ford's top executive. After his retirement Henry Ford II served on the company's board of directors and as chairman of the finance committee until his death on 29 September 1987.

Under Philip Caldwell's guidance, the Ford Taurus project was implemented, but by the time Taurus was released, Caldwell had retired as chairman of the board and chief executive officer. On 1 February 1985, he was succeeded by Donald Peterson, a Ford veteran with over 25 years' experience. Peterson had served as president and chief operating officer during Caldwell's tenure as chairman. Known throughout the auto industry as a 'car man,' Peterson had helped Caldwell bring the Taurus project to fruition and was committed to carrying out Ford's vision for the future.

The Taurus project was a tremendous success. It revolutionized worldwide automotive design and helped Ford outearn GM for three years running. Also during this era, the company diversified, acquiring Jaguar, Britain's premiere automaker, in 1989. Ford also acquired The Associates, a consumer and commercial lender, to improve its growing Financial Services Group.

But as history has shown again and again, the auto industry is cyclical, and as Ford enters the 1990s, it is faced with falling sales and a recession. The falloff in sales and production began when Iraq invaded Kuwait in August 1990, and, as a result, earnings in 1990 were off 78 percent from 1989 levels.

Though the situation looks grim, Ford's leader during this time of trial is seasoned by adversity. Chairman Harold A 'Red' Poling, who succeeded Donald Peterson in March 1990, ran Ford's North American operations during the early 1980s and helped save the company by ruthlessly cutting costs. 'I see us in a period of consolidation,' Poling explains.

Right: *The all-new 1991 Escort represents Ford Motor Company's blueprint for the future as a competitor in the global automotive industry. The Escort redesign program utilized Ford's resources around the world, from engine manufacturing at the Dearborn, Michigan plant to platform development at Mazda facilities in Japan (which is 25% owned by Ford).*

Opposite, top: *The Mercury Capri also has an international heritage. It was designed in Italy and built in Australia.*

'Once you've been through it before, you simply decide on the actions that need to be done and get on with it.'

Ford's plans for the future emphasize customer service, declaring 'If quality was the auto industry's obsession in the 1980s, customer service is clearly the challenge of the 1990s.' As competition intensifies Ford Motor Company believes the big winner in the decade of the 1990s will be the automaker who can 'pull away from the pack' in the treatment and handling of customers—before *and* after a car has been purchased. Lee R Miskowski, general manager of the Ford Parts and Service Division, believes that 'Ford's commitment to customer satisfaction will be as significant to our success in the 1990s as the aero look was to the turnaround in the 1980s.'

Above: *The Escort family for 1991, from top to bottom: the GT, the two-door hatchback, the four-door wagon and the four-door hatchback.*

Opposite above: *The Explorer is Ford's entry in the booming compact utility vehicle market.*

Opposite below: *The Mercury Topaz, a family car for the 1990s.*

Ford has established a number of programs that it believes will give the company a competitive edge in the 1990s. The first is a new national Customer Assistance hotline, with its toll free number (1-800-392-FORD). The service handles requests for information on products, explanations on warranty policies and any other question a customer may have.

Ford has also developed the Service Bay Diagnostic System—SBDS—a computer diagnostic system loaded with artificial intelligence. Designed to be user-friendly for technicians, SBDS is expected to improve significantly the ability of Ford and Lincoln-Mercury dealerships to repair vehicles.

Another tool that is proving invaluable in keeping Ford and Lincoln-Mercury dealership technicians current with the explosion of high-tech changes to new vehicles is OASIS—On-Line Automotive Service Information System. This computer-based system provides two-way communication between dealership service technicians and Ford.

Ford's commitment to customer service is only part of the reason that it continues to outperform its Big Three rivals. Its factory operations in the United States are far more efficient than GM's, and Ford's product lineup and financial position remain far stronger than Chrysler's.

INDEX

Below: *A 1958 Ford Fairlane 500 Sunliner convertible. The Sunliner had a traditional soft convertible top, but the Fairlane 500 was also available in the Skyliner configuration which featured a retractable hard top.*

The model below, *assembled at the Ford Long Beach plant, sports a Torch Red and Colonial White paint treatment and is equipped with a 352-ci (5.8-liter) V8 engine.*

PHOTO CREDITS

Above: *A rear-view of the 1955 Ford Fairlane Sunliner convertible. It's powered by a peppy 292-ci (4.8-liter) V8 engine and equipped with a Fordomatic transmission.*